Don:
" Tight lines; Silver Smiles"

# ISLAND FLY FISHERMAN

Vancouver Island

*Robert H Jones*

*Cary E. Whyte*

# ISLAND FLY FISHERMAN

## Vancouver Island

*Edited by*
*Robert H. Jones and Larry E. Stefanyk*

HARBOUR PUBLISHING

Harbour Publishing Co. Ltd.
P.O. Box 219
Madeira Park, BC
V0N 2H0
www.harbourpublishing.com

Edited by Robert H. Jones and Larry E. Stefanyk
Design by Andy Fenrick
Cover Photograph by Janice M. Stefanyk
Printed and bound in Canada

Harbour Publishing acknowledges financial support from the Government of
Canada through the Book Publishing Industry Development Program and the
Canada Council for the Arts, and from the Province of British Columbia through
the British Columbia Arts Council and the Book Publisher's Tax Credit through
the Ministry of Provincial Revenue.

**Library and Archives Canada Cataloguing in Publication**

Island Fly Fisherman : Vancouver Island / edited by Robert H.
Jones & Larry E. Stefanyk.

ISBN 1-55017-400-2

1. Fly Fishing—British Columbia—Vancouver Island.
I. Jones, Robert H., 1935-  II. Stefanyk, Larry E., 1949-
SH572.B8I84 2006          799.1'24097112          C2006-901475-2

## DEDICATION

To the Pacific Salmon Foundation, streamkeepers, community hatcheries, rod and gun clubs, fish and game protective associations, and all of the individual volunteers who put so much time, effort and money into helping our Island fisheries.

# TABLE OF CONTENTS

# ACKNOWLEDGEMENTS

My thanks to Larry Stefanyk, publisher of *Island Fisherman Magazine*, for agreeing to take on this project, and to the contributing authors, Vancouver Islanders all. They were chosen because their knowledge and experience has earned them the respect of brother and sister fly fishers here on the Island and beyond. A couple who accepted the challenge with trepidation because they did not consider themselves writers actually surprised themselves, but not me.

Robert H. Jones
*Courtenay, BC*

I wish to thank all of the contributing photographers—Wayne Moss, Barry Petrie, Janice M. Stefanyk, Frank Dalziel, Charlie Cornfield, Robin Pike, Kevin Reid and Robert H. Jones, who also supplied the fly photographs. I would also like to point out that this book would not have been possible without Bob's careful, painstaking editing. He maintains that an editor's sole purpose in life is to make writers look as good as possible to the readers, but I know how many long days he devotes to making it happen.

Larry E. Stefanyk
*Campbell River, BC*

# FLY FISHING VANCOUVER ISLAND

The term "fly fishing" on Vancouver Island has many meanings. One can be a stillwater fly fisher who concentrates only on lakes, or a river specialist who prefers that trout be caught only from moving water. Then there are winter-run steelhead fanatics who brave icy water and winter chill, dredging their flies deeply in a river's flow as blood congeals in their extremities. Others prefer summer-run steelhead because they are far more active, both in feeding and in the fight that follows a successful take. These same anglers are most likely to be found on the rivers when the salmon are running, whether it be small trout-like pinks, chrome-bright coho, massive chinooks or hook-jawed chums.

Add to these the saltwater fanatics, who are also divided into two groups. Beach fly fishers have been around for many decades, mostly on the Island's east coast, where they cast from shore for cutthroat trout, pink salmon and coho.

Inshore saltwater fly fishing is relatively new. Although practiced by a few for many years, it was given a sudden boost in the mid-1990s when Weigh West Marine Resort in Tofino introduced fly fishing packages for their guests. Key to the almost instant success was the combination of providing boats that were specially designed for fly fishing, the huge expanse of Clayoquot Sound that is sheltered from the open Pacific, and an abundance of coho.

As if having this wide range of fishing opportunities were not enough, thanks to relatively moderate temperatures Island fly fishers can indulge themselves virtually throughout the year—and a fair number of diehards actually do.

The nine contributors to this book have experienced it all, and between them have over 400 years of fly fishing experience. We trust that you will read what we have to offer, enjoy it and learn enough to make your own fly fishing experiences more fruitful and pleasurable.

**Larry E. Stefanyk**
*Publisher of Island Fisherman Magazine*

# CHAPTER ONE

*Pontoon boats are excellent for making quiet, stealthy approaches in shallow water.*

# FRESHWATER FISHING
# PLATFORMS *by Larry E. Stefanyk*

Vancouver Island has a wealth of lakes—nearly 700 ranging in size from tiny mountain tarns to large bodies of water like Kennedy, Cowichan, Upper Campbell and Nimpkish. Unfortunately, boat rentals are non-existent on all but a few on the southern Island and Saltspring Island that happen to have fishing resorts on their shores. This means that anglers must provide their own means of flotation or cast from shore. What best to choose? Well, while no one boat will serve all purposes, a few manage to come fairly close.

For big lakes it's not a stretch to simply employ relatively large, seaworthy boats like those used for fly fishing on saltwater. One of the most common for offshore is the 17–foot Boston Whaler Montauk, or one of various clones of these popular cathedral-hull vessels that have evolved over the years.

*When the ocean is storm tossed and rivers are flooding, nothing beats the peace and quiet of a lake.*

They are functional, safe, stable, manoeuvrable, and large enough to be comfortable, yet transportable enough for one person to easily launch or haul out. Depending on their configuration—with a centre or side console, or steering from the stern seat—they might be powered with outboard motors ranging from 40 to 100 or more horsepower, and may have something in the 10–15 h.p. range as an auxiliary motor.

*Two anglers can cast their flies easily from an open, uncluttered boat like this Boston Whaler.*

Another point in favour of this shallow-draft style of boat is that it can be launched in barely six to eight inches of water—which is often the case at small, unpaved boat ramps. This is assuming, of course, that the tow vehicle is a four-wheel drive.

While boats of this size easily carry three or four people, for the sake of safety from flying hooks only two should cast at any given time. The stability provided by the wide cathedral hull means that fly fishers can usually stand comfortably while casting, retrieving and fighting fish.

*Some of the most adaptable boats are constructed from lightweight aluminum. They can be used on large and small lakes, and for inshore saltwater fishing.*

It is probable that 12– to 14–foot aluminum boats make up the largest component of our inshore saltwater fleet, and they all do equally as well on lakes. Being light in weight they are easily towed, and can usually be launched at the crudest of ramps. Another plus in their favour is they can be rowed on lakes that do not allow motors.

Two anglers should be the maximum, and whether or not one or both may stand will depend entirely on variables as wide-ranging as the boat's hull shape and stability to an individual angler's age, agility and sense of balance. Some 14–foot boats are quite stable, while others are anything but. With 12–footers, remaining seated is usually the safest option.

Cartoppers usually fall in the 10– to 12–foot range and, as the name implies, they are light enough to carry on a roof rack or in the back of a pickup with the tailgate lowered. Most will easily handle two anglers, but due to space limitations they must work in concert with each other. A plus in favour of cartoppers is that they can be carried or dragged short distances to launch where no ramp is available.

Punts designed specifically for one person—common throughout the BC Interior, Cariboo and Chilcotin—are appearing more frequently on Island lakes. Constructed from aluminum, fibreglass or plywood, they range in lengths from 8 to 10 feet. The width and depth may vary, but they are usually a minimum of four feet at the widest point, almost always have a flat bottom, and contain an abundance of flotation material. These lightweight craft are easily rowed, and are amazingly

*Everything required for a full day of fly fishing on a lake is loaded into Jack Shaw's eight-foot-long punt.*

fast when powered by even a small electric motor.

Possibly the most famous fly fishing punt in BC was owned by the late Jack Shaw of Kamloops, a fly fishing pioneer and best-selling author. The amount of equipment that he packed into his 8–footer was astonishing, but once afloat he never had any reason to go ashore until his long day's fishing was done. His close friend and fishing companion for several decades, Ralph Shaw (no relation), had a

*Ralph Shaw fishing out of his punt.*

similar punt when he moved from Kamloops to Courtenay in the early 1980s. I use the past tense "had" because he has since modified it by having it shortened to just under eight feet, so it will fit inside a pickup truck box. He then mounted a single wheel on the bow and removable handles on the stern, which allow him to move the punt around like a large wheelbarrow. Once in the water, the wheel flips up and out of the way, and the handles are removed from the stern and stored until needed again. And

*Canoes offer a lightweight option for lakes, rivers and even inshore saltwater use.*

like his friend and mentor's famous punt, Ralph's is usually loaded to the gunwales with equipment whenever he sets out.

Canoes remain popular with some anglers. Depending upon their length, design and the material used in their construction, they range from featherweight aluminum shells capable of carrying one person to hefty fibreglass or wooden freighters that easily handle four people and are best propelled with an outboard motor. One of the most popular with anglers is the venerable 14–foot Sportspal, which is fashioned from lightweight aircraft-grade aluminum, carpeted throughout with buoyant Ethafoam, and has a large Ethafoam sponson on each side for added flotation and stability.

Robert H. Jones, editor of *Island Fisherman Magazine* (and this book), has owned one for 35 years. He told me that he and a friend once tried to intentionally capsize his Sportspal (they were in bathing suits at the time), but the sponsons made it virtually impossible. The best they could do was swamp it, "and we had to work at that," he concluded. At a total weight of about 37 pounds it's easily carried, and will support three passengers.

Inflatable boats, pontoon boats and float tubes are commonly found

*Inflatable boats are available in a range of sizes and shapes that offer comfort and stability on the water.*

bobbing about on Island lakes, and the latter are often the solution to private property signs posted around urban lakes, which limit access to occasional footpaths. Rafts and pontoon boats are also used for fishing in rivers that are tough-going along the banks, or simply too deep in which to wade. While some anglers might grumble about "rubber hatches" cluttering up the rivers, in the hands of one who is skilled at rowing and reading the current, rafts and pontoon boats are actually quieter and less disturbing than someone wading, and they have little, if any, disruptive effect on spawning fish and their redds or on the peace and quiet of anglers on shore.

Fifty years ago "inflatable" meant an oval or egg-shaped craft that was usually of war-surplus vintage. From these basic, clumsy, uncomfortable vessels have evolved some of the most versatile fishing platforms available. They offer portability, light weight, speed, safety and stability, plus the added attraction of requiring little "long term" storage space.

When it comes to size and shape, inflatables offer an amazing range of categories; from 20–foot-long, rigid-hulled hybrids used for rescue and fisheries enforcement work on the open ocean, to circular or U-shaped float tubes propelled by swim-fins or flippers on the occupant's feet.

The carrying capacity of an inflatable is about two to three times that of a similar-sized traditional boat. Depending on the construction and size of the air chambers, a 12–footer can support from 1,200 to 1,700 pounds. Aluminum cartoppers of equivalent length are rated at 350 to 600 pounds.

A common misconception is that an inflatable will sink if punctured. In this unlikely event, there is still plenty of flotation as they are comprised of several individual chambers. Unlike vehicle tires, inflatables rely on air volume rather than high pressure—usually about 1½ to 2 pounds per square inch. Thus, a punctured chamber will deflate slowly rather than blow out like a tire, and the rapid application of a simple duct tape patch will usually stem the flow of leaking air until a permanent repair is made.

Inflatables do have an annoying habit of expanding and contracting due to temperature and elevation changes. A boat pumped to proper rigidity at high noon on a hot day will sag noticeably in the cool night air, and vice versa. Also, a boat pumped up at a low elevation will be drum tight if taken to a lake at a much higher altitude.

Inflatables of interest to anglers come in five basic configurations: dinghy, kayak, sportboat, pontoon boat and float tube. Dinghies are either oval or U-shaped, and lack extended stabilizers at the stern. Rather than rigid floorboards they depend on tubular-shaped air chambers to provide moderate rigidity, and range in lengths from lightweight

8–footers to sturdy 20–foot river rafts. They are a good choice for use in rivers where rough water, swift currents and rocks are encountered. Combining low air pressure with material of high tensile strength, an inflatable absorbs collisions with rocks, even those with sharp edges. Should the craft swamp, the air chambers provide more than enough buoyancy to support the passengers. If an occupant is thrown overboard, it is far easier to crawl back over the side into an inflatable than with a standard boat.

*By using an external rod holder, a kayak becomes an efficient fishing platform that is swift and silent.*

Because of their hull configuration and lack of a keel, dinghies have poor handling qualities in wind and waves. Their most dangerous trait is a tendency for the bow to lift while heading into waves against an oncoming wind. Under this set of circumstances, a sudden surge of motor power might cause a dinghy to rear up and flip over backwards.

Kayaks are of similar construction to dinghies, but narrower and longer—usually about 11 to 12 feet. Propelled by a double-bladed paddle, they are faster and easier to control than rowed dinghies, but the occupant is confined to sitting. If used for fishing, they must be properly set up to secure the rod(s) in outside holders.

Lightweight "back packers" suitable for use on protected waters and in some cases slow-moving, obstacle-free streams, are usually of the small dinghy or kayak configuration. Because of its strength and flexibility, unreinforced PVC is the most popular material used. Generally, the larger the boat, the thicker the PVC. Some 8–footers weigh as little as 15 pounds. Although quite capable of supporting two persons, they are cramped because the side and floor air chambers take up much of

*Larry E. Stefanyk lake fishing out of his float tube.*

the interior. By opting for something around 9 to 10 feet long, weight increases accordingly—20 to 30 pounds—but so does its capacity, leg room and comfort.

Sportboats are the least portable of the inflatables, much more expensive, and because of their size, configuration and assembled components are usually trailered. They also range up to 20 feet long and generally incorporate rigid floorboards, a spray dodger, motor bracket, seats and a steering console. The main air chambers on both sides extend back beyond the transom, creating stubby, cone-shaped tails. These provide increased support for heavy outboard motors, plus improve the fore and aft stability. These are the most comfortable of the inflatables, and standing to cast or fight fish should prove no problem.

When it comes to float tubes and pontoon boats, Manitoba trout guru Bob Sheedy goes back to the early days of their introduction. In his excellent book, *Lake Fly Fishing Strategies*, he offers a wealth of in-depth information on how to choose and use float tubes, along with the best waders and swim fins to go with them. Following are some paraphrased excerpts from what Bob advises in much greater detail in his book, which is available at www.mwflyfishing.net.

*Propelled by oars, swim fins or an electric motor, pontoon boats are safe, efficient modes of travel.*

Float tubes are available in two basic configurations—circular and U-shaped. The former is most economical and generally uses a 20– or 22–inch truck inner tube for the air chamber, while a U-tube usually has a seamless bladder. The latter is easiest to enter and exit, and travels through the water with less drag.

Characteristics and features that either style should have in common:

- A heavy, sun-resistant nylon cover manufactured with double reinforced stitching. The zipper should be of a heavy-duty composite material that is "self-repairing"—if it pops due to expansion of the air chamber, simply bleed off a bit of air, then fully open and close the zipper to reseat it.
- Large, preferably compartmentalized pockets for storing lunches, fly boxes, cameras, raincoats and so forth.
- A large apron that can hold up to 80 feet of sinking line without tangling. Preferably, it should incorporate a ruler along the front edge for measuring fish.
- D-rings for backpacking and attaching accessories.
- Side handles for picking up the tube while walking into or out of the water.
- A fairly high, comfortable backrest to deflect waves and spray.
- A second internal tube for safety. This is a "must." Most setups use a motorcycle tube in the backrest for this. No backup tube, no sale.
- Some seamless padding on the seat.
- Avoid bright colours except on the back, which should be a large patch of Day-Glo orange or red for visibility, with a phosphorescent and reflective strip sewn onto it in an "X" configuration for low light conditions.
- Avoid "add-ons" like extra Velcro patches, line cutters, tippet dispensers, drink holders and so forth, as they are notorious line snaggers.

Pontoon boats provide comfortable mobility while retaining most of the stealth characteristics of a float tube *(assuming that you row quietly)*. Most have ample cargo space in pockets or modular clip-on racks, and large stripping aprons that accommodate any amount of line. These

*Those who know rowboats appreciate the ease of rowing a clinker-built. Roomy and stable, they are comfortable fly-fishing platforms.*

are "triple-threat" outfits in that they can be rowed, propelled with swim-fins, or powered by an electric motor—often all three are used interchangeably during a day of fishing.

Unlike a float tube, you can't toss a pontoon boat inside your car while it's assembled and inflated; in fact, some won't even fit into the back of a short-box pickup truck unless the tailgate is down. Nor do they backpack easily while assembled and inflated, and definitely not when there is an electric motor and full-sized, deep-cycle battery involved.

Long pontoons provide the best flotation and stability, but they don't turn as fast or easily as short ones, which is essential when working in fast water or shallows. For use on larger lakes where oars or a motor are used more often than swim fins, opt for long floats; otherwise, consider the more manoeuvrable blunt, banana-shaped pontoons. Avoid foot brace configurations that form a solid bar in favour of two-piece braces that fold out of the way when not in use. Get a solid, padded seat and be certain that it also has padded armrests on each side.

While no single fishing platform will serve all of the situations and freshwater conditions found on Vancouver Island and the Gulf Islands, probably the inflatable family comes closest, with a float tube by far the most economical and versatile. On even the smallest of urban lakes or remote mountain tarns an angler can fly fish easily from a float tube, and then do precisely the same thing on the largest

*Small punts that can be rowed make dry, comfortable fishing platforms on small lakes and, weather and water conditions permitting, can even be used on larger lakes or for close inshore saltwater fly fishing.*

of lakes by simply driving to a specific area and fishing close to shore. But when it comes to overall comfort, it's hard to beat those large, stable boats that must be trailered. It's all about what best serves your purpose and meets your needs, and of course, what you can afford.

The founder and publisher of *Island Fisherman Magazine*, **Larry E. Stefanyk** is also a well-known water colourist and print maker. He started fly fishing and tying flies while growing up in Alberta, and still devotes as much time to both as his busy schedule permits.

# CHAPTER TWO

*The low rod tip indicates that author Ralph Shaw is fishing a chironomid "wet line" style. Note that his punt is anchored at both ends for stability.*

# LAKE FLY FISHING ON VANCOUVER ISLAND *by Ralph Shaw*

When we moved from Kamloops, BC, to Courtenay in 1983, I brought with me 35 years of experience in lake fly fishing. This included my preference in types of flies, successful methods of fly fishing, and a belief that all would be the same on Vancouver Island. I was only partly correct …

My initial fly fishing experience was for coastal cutthroat trout on Middle Quinsam Lake, southwest of Campbell River. It was early April, and the first thing I noticed was that an active chironomid hatch was taking place. My choice was to use a Gold-Rib Chironomid pattern that came close to matching the hatch, and a medium slow-sinking line on my 5–weight rod.

*Gold-Rib Chironomid*

My companions, two dedicated worm fisherman, each had a large garden hackle dangling beneath his bobber. A few remarks were made about my choice of fly, which was small and nondescript looking; however, their comments turned to surprise when I started hooking fish on virtually every cast, and quite soundly out-fished both of them.

This exercise led me to believe that all was well, and my Interior fly fishing methods would continue to be successful. I was wrong. When my success ratio levelled out between mediocre and skunked, I came to appreciate that while much is the same, some things are very different and had to be addressed.

One variable is the species mix. In the southern Interior, two species make up most fish populations—rainbows and brook trout. On Vancouver Island, the primary species are coastal cutthroat and rainbow trout, but some lakes also have native kokanee and Dolly Varden. Rainbows (and in some cases, steelhead progeny) have also been introduced in many lakes that were either barren or held only cutthroats. Brown trout, smallmouth bass and yellow perch have been introduced in several South Island lakes, and browns are also present in one tiny lake on the North Island.

The provincial government lake-stocking program favours rainbow trout because they are easy to produce in hatchery facilities. I suspect we will see a growth in lakes stocked with rainbows,

*Coastal cutthroat trout*

which has implications for fly fishing in the future. Rainbows of all sizes will feed on the various stages of insect life, whereas once cutthroats gain some heft they become almost totally piscivorous. Thus, if fishing chironomids in a cutthroat lake, you can expect to catch small fish. To interest large ones, switch to a pattern that mimics a three-spined stickleback or better yet, a small kokanee or trout.

*Larry E. Stefanyk with a prime rainbow trout taken on a Black Articulated Leech.*

# A Geography Lesson

One has to be impressed with the size and diversity of Vancouver Island lakes. Generally, "island" conjures visions of a fairly small piece of land surrounded by water. In this case, perhaps "Vancouver Land" would have been a better name to describe its sheer land mass—which covers an area of 33,721 square kilometres (12,814 sq mi). Consider also that 19 Island lakes exceed 400 hectares (988 acres) in size. The largest is Kennedy Lake, near Ucluelet, which is over 6,400 ha (15,800 acres), and a close second is Cowichan Lake at 6,128 ha (15,100 acres).

The geography of the Island's mountain ranges sets many of the larger lakes located in valleys between steep-sided mountains, making them long and relatively narrow—up to 40 km long and 2 or 3 km wide. Some offer excellent angling while others like Nimpkish on the North Island and Kennedy have limited opportunities due to almost constant winds. It is worth noting that while fishing any of the big lakes, it pays to keep an eye out for strong thermal winds created by rising temperatures during the middle of the day.

*Although small Island lakes are often glassy calm, large lakes like Nimpkish and Kennedy can get too rough for safe fishing from boats.*

*Maple Lake, located midway between Cumberland and Courtenay, is typical of the Island's urban lakes that are stocked with rainbows, some of which grow to respectable sizes.*

Limited access is also a problem in some cases, and a few like Upper Campbell and Comox are dammed for hydroelectric power, creating great variations in water depth and shoreline access during periods of drawdown.

My point is that Vancouver Island is big. It offers nearly 700 lakes varying in size from those previously mentioned down to small tarns of less than four hectares (10 acres). To get a real appreciation for the size of this island, drive on modern blacktop from Victoria to Port Hardy in one day. You will drive past sparkling lakes right beside the highway (all contain trout), over rushing rivers and between towering mountains, and it will take you seven or eight hours depending on your respect for speed limits.

Since its early days of settlement, the Island's primary industry has been logging, as is still the case. The reason there are thousands of kilometres of roads is to move logs, a fact that leads to many restrictions concerning road use. Private forests in the southeast half of the Island have very restricted access to lakes west of the new freeway from Victoria to Campbell River, but the North Island is under tree farm licences, so public access is much more open.

Then there are the urban lakes, with some very popular and productive ones situated in downtown areas of Victoria and Nanaimo. Over 40 small lakes

*Bald eagle*

have boat restrictions: some do not permit power boats, others allow only electric motors, and a few have maximum speed limits. All are especially nice for fly fishing for they are peaceful, quiet places to while away a day in the company of herons, eagles, loons, kingfishers and other assorted wildlife.

## WEATHER CYCLES & FLY PATTERNS

Our lake fishery is somewhat unique in that those lakes at lower elevations offer excellent opportunities 12 months of the year. You can actually fish throughout the winter without chopping holes in the ice; however, if you simply must freeze while fishing, you can certainly do so in higher elevation lakes.

*Red-ribbed Peacock*

*Green Woolly Bugger*

Come February, wet line fishing with chironomids, bloodworms and leeches begins. While the Interior is still blanketed under ice and snow, chironomids are emerging in low elevation Island lakes. Then, as the sun starts coming back, lakes begin stirring with activity in the shallow bays and shoals. Plan on fishing during the warmest part of these winter days for best results.

*Black and Gold-Ribbed Chironomid*

My personal addiction is using a slow-sinking line for chironomid fishing, but floating lines and strike indicators probably have a higher success rate among beginning anglers. The good part is that both systems work.

My choice of patterns on some lakes starts with those incorporating black and gold, pheasant brown, and bright red. If you don't get any action, never hesitate to change pattern—often if need be. When fishing by yourself, try hanging a line over the stern with a Bloodworm attached—but make certain the rod is secure or you risk losing it if a good fish takes your fly.

*Pheasant Brown Chironomid*

*Red Chironomid*

*A proven fish catcher, the versatile Tom Thumb is the most popular dry fly in British Columbia.*

*Lightly-weighted patterns like this Purple Micro Leech are often the key to success.*

Wet-line anglers can stick with whichever patterns work in early February by simply moving up in elevation to higher lakes as the weather warms. Theoretically, you can have great chironomid action right up until midsummer, then in the fall as temperatures cool, you need only reverse the process and move systematically back to lower lakes. You can then continue fishing a fall cycle of these important sources of trout food, which exist in prodigious numbers.

As warmer weather approaches, the variety of insects hatching accelerates. From early April, hatches of mayflies, caddis and chironomids signal dry fly times. It may sound simplistic, but my most important dry fly is the Tom Thumb, which I tie in sizes ranging from no. 18 all the way up to a very large no. 6 on 1x or 2x hook lengths. This basic fly of deer hair can be adapted to meet a whole range of insect offerings. It is a superb sedge imitation when retrieved rapidly, simulating the speed of a traveller sedge—but hold onto your rod. To emulate emerging chironomids, a no. 16 floats on the surface in a perky manner that is deadly on feeding trout.

When casting near a shoreline with overhanging branches, a Tom Thumb works wonders at replicating several varieties of insects. Late in the evening, when big fish come into the shallows to feed, a no. 6 will continue doing well into the fading light.

*A shoreline with thick foliage and overhanging tree branches often adds terrestrial insects to the diet of fish—great places to try a Tom Thumb.*

Even though this is a period for dry flies, remain aware that nymph patterns of all insects will also work well on wet lines during this time of the year.

I have had excellent results fishing leeches in lakes of all sizes, and also in beaver-dam ponds. Trout have a season-long appetite for leeches, so whenever things are tough put one on and you may be pleasantly surprised at the result. Casting a leech into shallow water and then retrieving it with rhythmic pulses into deeper water is an effective method of wet-line fishing. Leeches are also good searching patterns, which work well when slowly mooched or trolled with a wet line along the

25

*A Black Woolly Bugger is one of my favourites.*

edges of shoals. They are a universal pattern tied in a variety of styles, colours and sizes—and virtually all of them work.

Dragonfly and damselfly nymphs are important patterns that work effectively for smallmouth bass as well as trout. It is my experience that big cutthroats like big patterns, and in this respect they differ from rainbows, which will take small patterns as well as larger ones.

## LOCATION, LOCATION, LOCATION...

For purposes of this chapter, let's consider lakes between 40 and 400 ha (100 and 1,000 acres) as "medium sized," which covers several hundred lakes on the Island. Because of their size, they tend to have more bays and protected shoals that make for good trout feeding grounds.

*Pontoon boats and float tubes are the choice of many Island fly fishers.*

26

Fly fishing the big lakes becomes a challenge when using small punts, pontoon boats or float tubes, which are the craft of choice for much of our fishery. Few places rent boats on Island lakes, so be prepared to supply your own.

*Doc Spratley is one of the old standbys of trolling flies.*

The prime places to fish big lakes are near river mouths, in protected bays, and at the outlets. River mouths are important sources of food, and the shoals in front of them can be very productive. Where they exist, narrows can also be fecund. First, look for obvious structures that serve as places to gather bait and concentrate on these locations—small islands, points of land, exposed weed beds, docks and bridges.

Depth sounders are becoming increasingly important tools to the fly fisher. In his excellent book *Lake Fly Fishing Strategies*, noted fly fishing guru Bob Sheedy points out that the most important use of a fish finder is to locate underwater structure rather than indicate fish. This is true in any lake, but especially so in large ones.

Trolling flies is practised on many lakes, and while I have had good cut-throat success with this method, I consider it fishing with a fly rather than fly fishing. Although there is considerable shore fishing with bait on the Island lakes, fly fishing is rare because of trees growing right to the shoreline.

Boat launch sites are often limited to one or two locations, usually in association with simple campgrounds or picnic sites that are normally located off logging roads and are seldom very well developed.

Small lakes under 40 ha (100 acres) provide much of the fly fishing opportunities on the Island. Indeed, lakes under 20 ha (50 acres) receive a large portion of the stocking program, with some as small as 4 ha (10 acres) receiving annual releases of cutthroat and rainbow trout. Small lakes are my choice for chironomid fishing, or a quiet day of mooching leeches along the shoreline.

Finding fish in small lakes is made easy by the restricted size of the water body, and the ease of finding shoals that slope into deeper water. It can be like fishing in a soup bowl, because the deeper water tends to be in the middle. Be warned, however, that some tiny lakes hold very large trout.

In reading the current regulations for Vancouver Island, I note that 41 lakes are shown as being regularly stocked. However, many are stocked that do not appear in the regulations. For up-to-the-minute information on stocking programs, check out the provincial website: http://www.env.gov.bc.ca/fw/.

High alpine lakes provide quality fishing, but hike-ins are necessary—some only a few minutes duration, others a few hours. Strathcona Park has several small, gin clear mountain lakes that have been stocked by volunteers and the government over the years. Their season is short, but they peak in late June, July and August when most low elevation lakes are in summer doldrums. Many of these lakes are accessible from Mount Washington Ski Resort.

When fly fishing from saltwater beaches, the open ocean and various rivers, Vancouver Island offers fly fishers a lifetime of challenges. However, it is those hundreds of lakes that create year-round opportunities in the quiet environs that are home to trout, char, smallmouth bass and other species that firmly entrench this island in the Pacific as a fly fishing paradise.

# POPULAR LAKE FLIES

*In the recipes offered here and elsewhere in this book, the name of the inventor and tier appears in brackets. If tied by someone else, the tier's name appears outside of the brackets.*

**Blood Leech**
*(Jack Shaw)*

**Hook:**  Mustad 9672, no. 10–4.
**Thread:**  Black.
**Tail:**  Clump of dark reddish-brown mohair with the thread removed. Tie in loosely at top of the bend.
**Body:**  Dark reddish-brown mohair tied in at tail. Wrap forward whilestroking fibres rearward. Tie off, cement, then brush hair to loosen it. Stroke hair so it is fairly flat along both sides, forming a top and bottom wing that flows smoothly back over the tail. Grip hook eye with a haemostat, dip fly in boiling water for a few seconds, then smooth wings rearward. After they dry, trim wings so they curve to meet the tail about a half-inch behind the bend.

**Turkey And Gold
Chironomid**
*(Jack Shaw)*

**Hook:**  Mustad 9671, no. 14–12.
**Thread:**  Black.
**Tail:**  Grouse feather fibres, sparse.
**Rib:**  Gold tinsel.
**Body:**  Turkey feather fibre.
**Shellback:**  Turkey strip.
**Thorax:**  Peacock herl.
**Bubble:**  White wool or acrylic.

## Bloodworm
*(Jack Shaw)*

**Hook:** 2XL nymph, no. 12–8.
**Thread:** Maroon.
**Tail:** Black bear hair.
**Rib:** Fine copper tinsel or
copper wire.
**Body:** Fine maroon chenille.
**Hackle:** Several cock pheasant rump fibres.

## Tom Thumb
*(Unknown) Ralph Shaw*

**Hook:** Mustad 9671, no. 16–8.
**Thread:** 8/0 black waxed UNI-
Thread for no. 16, 6/0
for no. 14–8 hooks. Wrap
rearward until even with
hook point, then back to centre.
**Tail:** Deer hair (late season is always best). Position small clump
on top of shank so tips extend one hook gap length beyond
the bend. Trim butts slightly ahead of centre and wrap
tightly back until even with hook point. Cement hair to
shank.
**Back/wing:** Deer hair clump about three times diameter of the tail.
Position so tips extend about 1½ to 2 shank-lengths
beyond the bend (this determines the wing's height). Hold
hair firmly in place and wrap forward. The butts should
spiral down around the shank, creating a ragged, uneven
body that aids in flotation. Make well-spaced wraps back
to the hook point, then forward to about ⅛–inch behind
the eye. Gather long hair together and fold forward to
form the back. Make two loose wraps around the hair and
shank, slowly draw tight, then make two tight wraps. Lift
hair tips up and back to form the wing, then wrap thread
under the front base to hold it upright. Form head, tie off
and cement. Trim any overly long hairs from underbody
but leave it fuzzy and ragged.

*Combining the right fly with the right tactic produced this fine rainbow for Ralph Shaw.*

*Ralph Shaw has made several modifications to his fly-fishing punt, including shortening it to 8 feet so it fits inside a pickup truck box, and adding a wheel at the bow that swivels up after launching. The two "wheelbarrow handles" at the rear are removable.*

A retired school principal, an Order of Canada recipient and an award-winning writer, **Ralph Shaw** resides in Courtenay, where his popular weekly outdoors column has appeared in the *Comox Valley Record* for over 20 years. He started dangling worms from a willow pole as a six-year-old growing up at Cold Lake, Alberta, over 70 years ago, and a few years later switched to crudely tied flies. There has been marked improvement in the quality of his tackle and fly-tying abilities since then.

# CHAPTER THREE

*Barry Petrie used a Black Leech pattern to tempt this rainbow from the slow-moving backwater of an Island river.*

# LEECHES ...
# THE "GO TO" FLY FOR
# ISLAND WATERS *by Robert H. Jones*

Most fly fishers have a favourite searching pattern that they use when testing new waters, and it's a good bet that many will be some variation of a leech. This is usually a good choice as leeches are found in most lakes and streams, and fish—especially trout and smallmouth bass feed on them heavily. A leech pattern can be so effective that some fly fishers state that using one is only a step above fishing with

live bait. I find it best to avoid these snobbish types, for their comments can get downright abusive at times—especially if you are catching fish and they are not.

Two nice things about leech patterns are that most are relatively easy to tie, and they are equally easy to fish with. Leeches have an undulating swimming motion, so creating and using patterns that simulate this movement makes good sense. For this reason a leech fly is usually long

*This cutthroat trout was hooked on a Beadhead Woolly Bugger while fishing out of a pontoon boat.*

and slender, widening toward the rear as does the real thing. I think it's fair to say that the Woolly Bugger in its various guises is probably the most popular leech pattern found in the ready-use boxes of fly fishers.

Black is by far the favourite colour, at least with anglers, but various shades of brown, olive, maroon and purple do exceptionally well at times. The late Jack Shaw of Kamloops, BC, once discovered a batch of "sad" maroon mohair at a local sewing and knitting shop. He purchased a hank and discovered that leeches tied with it produced strikes far above average. He promptly went back to the store and bought the entire batch, thereby driving other fly fishers in the area crazy because they could never quite match his particular leeches.

*Bead Head Woolly Bugger*

After I fell heir to one of Jack's leeches (thanks to Ralph Shaw, no relation), I used it as a guide to start experimenting with shredding and combing out various colours of acrylic yarn and blending it. Many weeks and hundreds of feet of yarn later, I wrote to Jack and told him which colours of yarn I had even-

*Jack Shaw's Blood Leech*

tually used to more or less match his fly. He later phoned to say that shortly after he discovered how well his "magic mohair" worked, he had studied it under a microscope to try determining why (which is why he was so successful as a fly tier and fisherman). "With the exception of your hot orange," he told me, "you have all of the same colours."

*Combed Acrylic Blood leech*

Combing and blending the yarn is time-consuming but not terribly difficult. All you require is a steel-bristled pet brush and a stee-toothed pet comb to separate the strands of yarn, which actually consist of fine filaments about four inches long. You also require a four– or five–inch length of wooden dowel around which to wrap the yarn to hold it with one hand as you brush it out with the other. I usually cut the acrylic in three–foot lengths and then wind all of the colours onto the holder at once. As the material is brushed out, lay it in small piles with the filaments running the same way. After accumulating several piles, use the steel-toothed comb to separate the filaments even further. You will eventually end up with three stacks of filaments about four, three and two inches long, plus a bunch of tight little balls of material that are best discarded. I keep the piles separated by length, and contained with a loop of acrylic yarn threaded through a small plastic bead. Simply insert the material inside the loop, then slide the bead against it to close and tighten the loop.

By combing different base colours of yarn together, an endless range of colours and shades can be achieved. A productive leech shade consists of the following colours in the number of strands shown: three maroon, two dark brown, one each of dark maroon, black, mauve, yellow, hot orange, cerise, robin's egg blue, dark purple. This material can also be cut into short pieces and mixed in a coffee blender, with or without dubbing enhancer. This is the colour that my friends usually scrounge from me most often.

Leeches are primarily nocturnal, but in stained waters like that found in Quennell Lake, leech patterns work fine at any time of day. This is also true in clear water at times, but in those cases the best periods are always morning and evening twilight. Experience will reveal that trout seem to favour small leeches during bright daylight hours, but in morning or evening low-light conditions, larger fish may take patterns up to four inches long.

Good places to try are on top of shoals or close to the bottom along the deeper edges. Leeches prefer areas with weeds or a bottom covered with detritus, probably for the concealment these conditions offer. It's when they leave these safe zones that they become most susceptible to hungry fish. Unlike insect or minnow hatches, which are fairly predictable, leeches are random targets of opportunity that are seldom ignored. I believe this is why they work so well as searching flies—while there

*Quennell Lake*

are certainly times and places where they work best, you can toss them almost anywhere at any time and stand a reasonable chance of connecting with a trout or bass.

In shallow water try a floating line, but for depths beyond five feet or so, switch to a slow-sink and give your fly time to reach bottom before retrieving. In deep water, of course, go to a faster-sinking line so you needn't wait as long for your fly to get down into the strike zone.

*This rainbow swims away after being fooled by a Micro Leech.*

A fairly slow hand-twist or short-strip retrieve of two to six inches, with occasional twitches of the rod tip, will provide the desired motion. However—and this might sound suspiciously like heresy—on occasion a sudden long strip or burst of speed might be just what it takes to trigger a take.

With rainbow trout in particular, the strike might range from an arm-jolting tippet-snapper to a gentle nip, for they can be notorious short-takers at times. For this reason, Jack Shaw recommended trimming the tail of his Blood Leech as short as a half inch past the hook bend. I found this puzzling, as most leech patterns call for a fairly long, sinuous tail; however, shortening the tail as instructed certainly does increase the strikes on short-takers.

Many tiers swear by marabou for their leeches, but I find that Root's Llama Hair also works, especially when blended with a touch of enhancer. Mohair is popular with many tiers, and for good reason, and as noted earlier, a few of my friends have joined me in using combed acrylic.

While tying a leech pattern, using a metal bead, cone or wraps of wire around the front of the hook shank will provide the desired up-down sinusoidal swimming action. If using a bead or cone, black or copper are good colours.

## LEECH FLIES

**Bead Head**
**Cat Fur Leech**
*(Jim Crawford)*

**Hook:** Mustad 94840, standard or 1XL, no. 8.

**Thread:** Black or brown. Use Kevlar or gel-spun polyethylene that wraps tightly.

**Bead:** Black tungsten or brass.

**Tail:** Marabou tips, black and brown—not too dense—about half the body length. Blend in a few strands of tiny black or red-black holographic Mylar. Tie in at hook bend.

**Body:** Wrap shank evenly with thread then coat with cement. Wrap material evenly around the tail binding so it trails halfway along the tail. Wrap another section at mid-shank, another at the bead. Tail should be wider than the head. If necessary, trim the body at top and bottom to flatten it.

**Note:** This is a variation of Kamloops tier Nick Solomon's Nick's Bead Head Leech. Jim's wife had a Norwegian forest cat that provided a perfect mix of browns, blacks and softness to match the long-strand, very soft wool used for the original. Alas, the cat has long since died, so Jim guards his dwindling supply of flies closely.

**Canada Blood Sucker**
*(Unknown) Mac Warner*

**Hook:** 3XL–4XL, no. 4–10.
**Tail:** Short tuft of fluores-cent red yarn.
**Body:** Medium black chenille (or colour of choice).
**Hackle:** Brown, palmered and clipped short.
**Head:** Taper thread from the body to hook eye for about ¼ of the shank length.

**Combed Acrylic Leech**
*(Robert H. Jones)*

**Hook:** Eagle Claw L058 3XL, no. 4–10.
**Bead:** Optional. Small black or copper.
**Weight:** Optional. Several wraps of lead wire around front ¼ of hook shank.
**Thread:** Maroon.
**Rib:** Fine gold or copper wire.
**Tail:** Small clump of leech blend, maroon or black acrylic yarn, combed out before tying in.
**Body:** Tie in one end of a small clump of acrylic and wrap forward counter-clockwise, tapering toward the head. Make fairly loose wraps at the rear, and tighter toward the front. Wrap the rib forward clockwise and tie down, then use a bodkin to tease the material out from between the wire.
**Sides:** Optional. 1 to 2 strands of black, brown or copper Flashabou on each side.

**Egg-sucking Rabbit Leech**
*(Doug Porter)*

Hook:    Mustad 36890, no. 6–4 for still-water, 3/0–6 for rivers.
Thread:   6/0 Orange.
Tail:     Black rabbit strip approximately ⅔ of the shank length.
Body:    Black rabbit strip wrapped around the shank.
Flash:    2 strands of pearl Flashabou tied along each side of the body.
Egg:      Fire orange chenille.

**Micro Blood Bugger Leech**
*(Brian Smith)*

Hook:    Mustad 9671, no. 10–12.
Thread:   Black UTC.
Tail:     Black marabou, webby is best.
Rib:      5–6 turns of gold rope.
Hackle:   Black saddle, 2 times the hook gap, palmered through the body, 2 turns at the head.
Body:    BC Blood Dazzle Dubbing.

**Mini Leech**
*(George Will)*

| | |
|---|---|
| **Hook:** | Mustad 9672, no. 12. |
| **Bead:** | Small black. |
| **Body:** | Combed out maroon Antron dubbing. Keep it thin and relatively sparse. |

**Rabbit Leech**
*(Unknown) Mac Warner*

| | |
|---|---|
| **Hook:** | Long shank, no. 6–10. |
| **Body:** | Black chenille. |
| **Wing:** | Strip of black rabbit the same length as the hook. |

**Spun Rabbit Hair Leech**
*(Mac Warner)*

| | |
|---|---|
| **Hook:** | Mustad 9672, no. 6–10. |
| **Thread:** | Brown or black. |
| **Tail:** | Small clump of rabbit fur. |
| **Body:** | Black or brown rabbit fur spun in a dubbing loop. Trim top and bottom flat but leave sides sticking out. |
| **Note:** | This is an excellent pattern where small leeches are present, usually in small lakes with stained water. |

*Author Robert H. Jones with a lingcod that couldn't resist his chartreuse and white Clouser Minnow (pattern on page 145).*

Courtenay resident **Robert H. Jones** edits *Island Fisherman Magazine*. He tied his first fly 60 years ago, and is said to have shown some slight improvement since.

# CHAPTER FOUR

*Careful preparation is a key step toward success in beach fly fishing for cutthroat trout.*

# BEACH FISHING FOR CUTTHROAT TROUT *by Kevin Reid*

Vancouver Island offers some amazing fly fishing opportunities, among which one of the most exciting and challenging is casting from the beaches for sea-run cutthroat trout. The reasons are simple: you need only a minimum of equipment, and those supercharged trout provide great sport for visitors and residents alike. I have been at it for 15 years or so, during which I have developed a "game plan" that has dramatically increased my rate of success.

Preparation is a key ingredient to having a pleasant, productive experience, and it requires good equipment. You must select appropriate tackle for the conditions where you intend to fish, which range from pinpoint casting to selectively feeding cutts in a sheltered estuary, to punching out long casts on open, windy beaches.

I prefer light tackle. My present outfit consists of a 10–foot, 5–weight G.Loomis rod, a no. 6 Tioga reel, Scientific Angler weight forward 4–, 5– and 6–weight floating lines, and 150 yards of backing.

*Not all beaches are sandy, so good wader boots are a must for walking on rocky shorelines.*

A 12–foot-long leader completes this basic setup, which will handle the varied situations encountered while chasing sea-run cutts. A 5– or 6–weight system provides enough backbone to fight and land everything from early spring 10–inch "brats" to late fall "yellow bellies" of up to five pounds. The heavier outfit punches casts into the wind with a more authority, and easily handles any pink salmon encountered during the summer months. You must work harder with a 5–weight outfit, but it can be done.

As reels are exposed to a salty, sandy environment, choose one constructed from anodized aluminum or graphite, with a smooth, easily adjustable drag system. Be sure it is well lubricated and in good working order before heading for the beach, and rinse it off with fresh water when you are done for the day. These simple precautions can add years of life and trouble-free performance to a reel being used in a marine environment.

A hat and polarized sunglasses are a must. My vest is loaded with the usual things like clippers, knife, a good selection of flies, floatant, needlenose pliers, sharpening stone, and (I can hear the purists screaming "God forbid!"), lead split shot. Also included are small spools of fluorocarbon tippet material down to 4–pound test, which can be very crucial to success. During intense light situations that are frequently encountered on sunny days, fishing a small diameter, virtually invisible leader is often the solution to getting shy fish to take the fly.

Beach fishing or, on some days, beach strolling, often means covering a lot of coastline to locate fish or their likely environment. Well-fitting boots with sturdy soles are a must to get you down steep access trails, and for walking across rocky beaches. Most modern waders will do the job and each material offers specific benefits. Neoprene products provide added warmth and flotation, which, combined with their affordability makes them a popular choice. Breathable "Gore-Tex" waders provide ease of mobility that is second only to wading wet, and are especially appreciated when making those long walk-ins that are often essential in finding private "beach all to myself" locations.

Now that we are dressed and have our tackle ready for a day of action, all we need is a beach and some fish—right? Well, no. Many other factors come into play. Gathering information beforehand is a great place to start. Talk to friends and acquaintances who may have been on the beaches recently, and check out local tackle shops for what's

*A good general rule is to start at an easily accessible estuary and then fish the adjoining beaches.*

been happening. This can be especially important during the spring, when downstream fry migrations are occurring. This is when the estuaries of small creeks are often overlooked in favour of large rivers, which frequently prove to get just a tad crowded.

Prioritize your search. Check areas with good vehicle access first and leave the walk-in locations for afterward. When in doubt, start at an estuary then walk the adjoining beaches. Be on the lookout for fish showing on the surface. Other wildlife often indicates holding fish. Shore birds feeding on baitfish provide obvious clues, for where there is bait there are usually larger fish feeding on them.

When approaching any beach, learn to recognize the smaller micro-environments within a given stretch of shoreline, and watch for signs indicating when you go from one microenvironment to another. For example: a sandy area with small stones is a good environment for shrimp, so try a shrimp pattern like a Handlebar Moustache or Frozen Shrimp. Patches of eelgrass hide baitfish like sandlance (needlefish)

and sticklebacks, so a Glass Minnow or Murray's Rolled Muddler should prove effective. Large rocks and boulders provide good habitat for euphausiid shrimp, so opt for small green patterns like a Perla or Mysid. Kelp forests often attract large schools of herring, so I always fish around the edges with a green Llama Hair Minnow in sizes 4–6.

*Good searching patterns are shrimp imitations like this Handlebar Moustache.*

When you learn to tell the difference between these environments and the types of bait they attract, this information indicates the appropriate size and colour of fly to use. Usually. After all, cutts, being trout, may occasionally decide to target one specific bait—whether or not it happens to be present.

Something I have noticed about most anglers is they become so focussed on the end of their line that many of the small, important things occurring around them are missed. I often fish for sea-run

*Although not usually considered fussy eaters, cutthroats can become downright picky at times. This is when it pays to experiment with the size and colour of a fly and its retrieve.*

*"Beach fishing" also includes probing well up into the estuaries, especially on incoming tides.*

cutthroats in late spring. During the first few seasons I had moderate success, but one day, at the very edge of my peripheral vision I saw some very small fish darting away every time I moved. I quickly recognized them as rather dark-coloured sticklebacks about a half-inch long. I recalled the words of Tom Murray, inventor of the Rolled Muddler: "Sticklebacks are the favourite food of sea-run cutthroat." I quickly changed flies and was into fish after fish. My point being: sometimes the bait sees you first. Keep your eyes on the water all around you for signs, however small. This tip alone will improve your fishing success on any water. It certainly did mine.

Your first few steps on a beach can tell you a lot about where to fish it. On my initial approach, I stop and watch for information that may help immediately, or come in useful later on. My first look around is always for birds. Ducks, herons, seagulls, cormorants and kingfishers almost always mark a source of baitfish, and sandpipers are known to feed on shrimp and other crustaceans.

I then look at the geography, making mental note of high spots or shoals, low spots or holes, boundaries of kelp beds or eelgrass. All of this information may help, especially on a rising tide. I always plan my retreat ahead of time, for on an incoming tide it's always better to err on the side of caution. Backing off a shoal should be done well before the water gets too deep. Swimming in chest waders is uncomfortable, embarrassing, and in some places downright dangerous.

Over the years, I have developed some other specific strategies for fishing different tidal scenarios. Starting with high tide, I find that points of land, no matter how small, offer a distinct advantage. They mark high spots that help in casting farther out to fish that might be well off an open beach at high tide. Casting from these high spots into deeper holes often finds fish holding in them, even if the difference in depth is only a few inches.

If fishing a beach for the first time, walk out onto the longest point of land and look back toward the bay for breaking or taller waves that identify shoals. Also look for eelgrass or kelp beds appearing on the surface. Try to determine which way the tide is flowing, then cast to any likely looking locations. Concentrate most of your effort on the high probability areas, but cover all of the available water by "fan casting" 180 degrees around your perch on the point.

Changing tides is where the game gets really interesting. On a falling tide you are forced into a "chasing" situation, for the trout are always moving away from you with the receding water. If you know that the beach follows a shoal and some connecting high spots, use this knowledge during a falling tide to always fish the deepest water available. Fish favour these deeper places as they offer more protection from airborne predators like ospreys and eagles.

The single most important thing about low tide is the opportunity to mentally map the beach. Observe the geography, identify potential holding spots, and determine where the best feeding environments are located. Also identify the type of structure—rocky outcrops, weed beds, sand bars, deep holes—as fishing their perimeters first will avoid

*As the tide recedes you must follow the fish out. This is a good time to check for the types of underwater structures that attract trout.*

*Two fly fishers at the Oyster River mouth have determined that the trout are feeding close to shore during an evening high slack tide.*

spooking any fish that might be feeding in that area. Low tide also yields clues regarding the types of bait available and its abundance.

Then, as the tide starts coming in around you, put all of this information into practice. The bait and trout will move in with the rising water, and having done your homework provides all of the clues required to be successful. Connect the now submerged high spots, make informed decisions on the feed available, anticipate where the fish will be, and then make your presentations accordingly.

The current direction and strength of its flow affects the fishes' behaviour. Trout are designed to face into the current, so presenting your fly "upstream" of your target and swimming it into their feeding zone makes good sense. It's been my experience that areas with strong tidal currents cause the fish to either cycle while searching for bait, or seek eddies or "soft water" in which to hold and wait for food to come to them.

Fishing an estuary and river mouth is always a great tactic for catching cutts. Casting across the current and drifting your fly to the 45 degree down-stream mark before beginning the retrieve is most effective. My most productive retrieve is a series of quick, three–inch jerks. That said, at other times a cross current swing with no retrieve at all can be very effective.

As fly fishing continues increasing in popularity, more anglers are showing up on the beaches in search of action. While some of the more popular areas get fairly crowded when pink and coho salmon are staging off the river mouths, relatively few fly fishers prospect the beaches for cutthroat trout during the rest of the year. When you do encounter someone, rest assured that he or she is a kindred soul, and probably well worth spending some time with while exchanging information, telling lies and swapping fly patterns.

After all, at times just talking about cutthroat trout fishing is as much fun as doing it. Well, almost ...

*Wayne Yoshizawa probing the waters of a beach near Campbell River.*

# BEACH FLY PATTERNS

### Frozen Shrimp
*(Kevin Reid)*

| | |
|---|---|
| **Hook:** | Eagle claw 1197, no. 1. |
| **Thread:** | Hot pink. |
| **Tail:** | 4 peacock sword herls. |
| **Body:** | Rear ⅔ holographic tinsel; front ⅓ hot pink Icicle Chenille. |
| **Wing:** | 4 strands pearlescent white Flashabou. |

### Murray's Rolled Muddler
*(Tom Murray)* **Bill Luscombe**

| | |
|---|---|
| **Hook:** | Mustad 9671 or 9672, no. 12–10. |
| **Thread:** | Red. |
| **Tail:** | Mallard flank, half the hook length, ¼-inch wide and folded lengthwise twice. |
| **Rib:** | Silver wire, counter-wound. |
| **Body:** | Silver tinsel. |
| **Wing:** | Mallard flank, ½-inch wide, folded lengthwise twice and-tied in so ends are even with tail ends. |
| **Head:** | Small clump of light brown deer hair, spun and clipped to an arrow shape, flat on the bottom. Leave a few hairs lying back to form part of wing. |

## Perla

*(Roderick Haig-Brown)*
*Art Lingren*

| | |
|---|---|
| **Hook:** | No. 8. |
| **Thread:** | Black. |
| **Rib:** | Oval gold tinsel. |
| **Body:** | Olive, primrose yellow, or lightgreen. |
| **Throat:** | Badger hackle or brown partridge. |
| **Wing:** | Section of golden pheasant tail feather mounted flat overbody. |

## Mysid

*(Roderick Haig-Brown)*
*Art Lingren*

| | |
|---|---|
| **Hook:** | No. 14–10. |
| **Thread:** | Black. |
| **Tag:** | Orange silk. |
| **Tail:** | 5 golden pheasant neck tippet feather fibres. |
| **Body:** | Flat silver tinsel. |
| **Throat:** | Blue hackle extending to hook bend. |
| **Wing:** | Barred wood duck flank feather. |

*Author Kevin Reid with a typical sea-run cutthroat from an estuary on the east coast of Vancouver Island.*

A resident of Miracle Beach, north of Courtenay, realtor **Kevin Reid** started fly fishing 30 years ago at age 11. A year later he received a fly-tying kit as a present, and has been diligently trying to develop "the perfect" fly ever since.

# CHAPTER FIVE

*A female summer-run steelhead.*

# ISLAND STEELHEAD *by Rory E. Glennie*

Free-flowing rivers demonstrate water in its loveliest form. The same simple beauty is also present in streams, brooks, rivulets, trickles and seeps—all miniature renderings of the grandest rivers. The common denominator is gravity; that water flows downhill while seeking its own level is elementary.

The geography and geology over which water flows determines the character of a particular watercourse. High gradient, boulder-strewn pocket water, as found on the Heber River; deep, rock-walled canyon pools like those on the lower Gold River; broad meandering flows cutting through low gradient, alluvial gravel deposits like stretches located on the Salmon River, are but three water types one might encounter on Vancouver Island. With a number of variations on these common themes—often found within the course of any given river—an angler seemingly confronts an unending puzzle of water types. However, upon closer investigation, there are really only a limited number of recurring themes. After all, given the confining laws of physics, water and gravity in combination can only perform certain physical tasks. Understanding those limitations aids an angler in the quest of catching fish.

*The Gold River's Peppercorn Pool is typical of larger Island waterways.*

Permit me to assume that you have a rudimentary understanding of river fly fishing, and some experience in catching a few fish from them. Although rank beginners might find some of what follows a bit confusing, it would take an entire book to bring neophyte fly fishers up to speed. Fortunately, there are several good works on the subject of fly fishing for steelhead available, and my advice is to check them out to learn what they have to offer. I suggest *Steelhead* by Barry Thornton (Hancock House) and *Steelhead*

*An example of a mid-sized stream is the Muchalat River on the Island's west coast.*

*Fly Fishing and Flies* by Trey Combs (Frank Amato Publications).

Of various resource materials available that will help you plan for a trip, most significant is a current issue of the Freshwater Fishing Regulations Synopsis published annually by the provincial Fisheries Branch. It is an important tool in understanding the complex regulations governing anglers and freshwater fisheries. In it you learn that you must obtain and carry with you a valid non-tidal angling licence, and the appropriate species stickers for the type of fish you wish to catch. Before going off on a much-anticipated river sortie, study the regulations. It can save you grief and frustration by revealing beforehand whether a certain stream has an angling closure, species non-retention regulation, boating restriction, or is a "classified water" that requires you to purchase an additional permit. A good working knowledge of the regulations also provides more comfort than simply guessing about whether or not you are fishing legally.

On Vancouver Island, the time of year largely dictates the race and type of steelhead for which you will be angling. Suffice to say that summer-run steelhead are best pursued from May until October, and winter-runs during the November to April time frame. Besides, wintertime stream closures are largely designed to protect summer-run steelhead from over-exploitation, so this fact alone may help to clear up any confusion.

# SUMMER-RUN STEELHEAD

It is summer-run steelhead that really make fly fishers sit up and take notice of what rich rewards coastal river fly fishing has to offer. A summer-run steelhead is a supercharged, sea-run rainbow trout that has fattened on the ocean's great bounty, and having returned to its home stream, is willing to rise to the surface to bite a feather and fur bauble in broad daylight. Almost limitless prose and several exhaustive tomes have been penned in honour of this great game fish, and I can add very little to what is already written. Search out the literature, study the methods and techniques, pore over maps to locate prospective waters and talk to anybody who has been to the streams—and not just fly fishers, for lure-chuckers and bobber-tossers can provide a wealth of knowledge, too.

*After a quick photograph, Ralph Shaw released this Quinsam River summer-run steelhead.*

Linking up with a skilful fly fishing guide for your first time out can be a shortcut that pays enormous dividends in the information gained. Any do-it-yourself adventures after that will likely be much more productive, and your personal skill level and knowledge base will be broadened immeasurably.

Determined, self-reliant fly fishers—those who have kicked up their knowledge and understanding of steelhead a notch or two by studying the greats may find that

*On large Island rivers like the Gold, Salmon, Stamp and Campbell, an inflatable raft is a great way to cover the best water.*

the best way to go about it is to simply get onto a river known to have a good run of summer fish, then set out exploring.

Two well-known waters that were favoured and written about by the late Roderick Haig-Brown are the Campbell and Heber rivers. The historic Islands Pools in the fly-fishing-only section of the Campbell have attracted summer-runs and fly fishers for a long time. Although the runs have diminished in number of late, hopes are they will eventually rebuild to former glory.

The Heber, a tributary to the Gold River, hosts a strong run of wild, naturally produced summer-runs. There is good access to the

*Low, clear water meant fine—and far off fishing—tactics, but the payoff for Kevin Reid was this Heber River summer run steelhead.*

*Tom McCulloch with a prime Oyster River winter-run steelhead. (Gerry Schad photograph.)*

river from Highway 28, which runs right beside the river for several kilometres. Beware! Those steelhead are spooky. The Heber's water is so clear that I swear those fish can see you coming from the time you pull out of your driveway to leave home. Be sure to dress in muted earth tones and move stealthily.

As a base, start searching for riffles and runs with large boulders on the bottom, preferably about knee-to-armpit deep, and flowing at what is best described as a comfortable walking pace. Cover the area with consecutive arcs of a sunken fly swinging slowly across and downstream. If there are no takers, try a bushy dry fly swung over the same water. Or vice versa.

The frothy-white water spilling into the head of a pool or run often holds a good fish under it. This steelhead is best tempted to the surface with a goodly-sized dry dangled along the bubble trail. As well, present the fly to any summer-runs you see laying beside boulders or rolling at the surface. Should that fail, go immediately to Plan B—seek a competent fly fishing guide.

# WINTER-RUN STEELHEAD

In my opinion, this is simply the toughest fly fishing challenge offered on coastal streams. Period. If there is any form of fishing that requires anglers to "pay their dues" by putting in countless long hours, often over many days, before obtaining grace with a hook-up from their quarry, winter steelhead fly fishing is it. The extraordinary concentration necessary to detect a steelhead subtly mouthing your fly is often thwarted by the harsh natural elements. A sullen, monochromatic backdrop of black, white and shades of grey lulls the eyes; frozen fingertips and icicles hanging from one's nose make physical reactions sluggish; flat-lighted, flowing water fixes the mind in a near-hypnotic trance; feet turn

*A spirited fight, a final photograph and the successful release of a Gold River winter-run steelhead.*

61

*Chrome bright and full of fight sums up this winter-run steelhead released by Jack Simpson.*

to lead from hours submerged in frigid water. Then, suddenly, all of this discomfort is forgotten by an electric jolt sent via the line to your entire body—a steelhead is suddenly on. That is the beauty and reward of winter steelhead fly fishing—instant resurrection.

Three fine Island rivers with good access to winter steelhead are the Cowichan, Gold and Salmon. Several other easily accessed rivers suffer from depleted runs, and many are subsequently closed to angling. Hopes are that these runs will eventually rebuild and fly fishing on them can again be pursued. Logging road and highway bridges cross each of these streams in a few places. Stopping to scope out a river's flow from a bridge can help plan your trip—whether to head farther upstream or down, depending on the water's clarity and quantity of flow.

Generally, not being one to stifle anyone's prerogative, I can't recommend starting out on your own by simply stumbling about blindly on a winter steelhead stream—but you have to start somewhere. Linking up with an experienced steelheader, however, may help kick-start the learning process. If he or she happens to be a fly fisher, all the better —but don't overlook going with the aforementioned lure-chuckers and bobber-tossers, for the exercise is aimed primarily at learning where and when to fish, not how.

As with summer-runs, much has been written about taking winter-runs with a fly rod. The same advice holds true for a prospective winter fly fisher: it pays to study the literature available and seek advice from knowledgeable anglers.

A good grounding in the basics of winter steelheading, and an understanding of specific run timing will save much useless flogging. Many of the same water types that hold summer steelhead will hold winters. The main practical difference is that winter-runs are notorious for hanging tough near the bottom. With the heavy flows of winter, one might wonder how a steelhead can hold so easily in such strong currents. It is much like the coating of fine dust that clings to the hood of your car while driving down the highway at 100 km/h—combined physics—the hydrodynamic shape of the fish and a thin layer of slower water down amongst the boulders. This aspect necessitates that a fly must be drifted almost into their face to elicit a strike. A heavyweight sink-tip line coupled by a short leader to a weighted fly—albeit not necessarily a large one—dead-drifted with the assistance of multiple line mends is in order. This scenario is best tackled through employing the benefits of a long, two-handed

*On wide, swift-flowing rivers like the Campbell, an inflatable raft provides a safe, stable platform for covering the water efficiently.*

Spey rod. Upon seeing the fly, the steelhead may follow it for a brief moment as it swings, then gently take it and sink back into its hold.

Notably, the biggest single factor in whether winter steelhead can be expected to move very far to take a fly is water temperature. Generally, warmer winter flows mean more active fish. Even when the water is quite low, they will occasionally follow a fly into thin water before grabbing it—or spook themselves back into deeper or more turbulent

*Barry Petrie with a prime winter-run steelhead taken on the lower Stamp River. His guide was Matt Guiget.*

cover water. When the fish seem more willing to move a bit to intercept or chase a fly, then that is the time to use lighter density lines, even floaters. Again, much has been written on this subject, and it is required learning if you want to aspire to proficiency in winter fly fishing. Should you become a winter steelhead fly fishing devotee, you will have joined a minority. And when you hook into your first winter-run fish, you will become an enlightened convert. After that, your fly fishing perspective will never be the same.

On the following pages are four very productive patterns that have become "must have" flies on any of my steelhead sojourns—two wet and two dry that should serve you well. Then, all that is left is to hunt up some steelhead and present your gift to them.

# STEELHEAD FLY PATTERNS

**Pink Polliwog**
*(Rory E. Glennie)*
For winter-run steelhead
holding on the bottom.

**Hook:** Mustad 9174,
no. 2.

**Thread:** Fluorescent pink
UNI-Thread or
Kevlar.

**Tail:** Pink/white
variegated chenille. Tie one end of a 2½ inch piece in at
the bend, untwist until the thread core is straight, then
untwist 4–6 times more. Place dubbing needle across the
middle and fold the tag end to the tie-in point, pinch
between thumb and forefinger, and remove the dubbing
needle. After the tail twists back on itself, tie it off.

**Body:** 4 pieces of pink Antron yarn with a single piece of black
or chartreuse yarn for the eye spot, spun and clipped to a
ballshape.

**Copperhead Leech**
*(Rory E. Glennie)*
For winter and summer
steelhead.

**Hook:** Mustad 9049,
no. 2–2/0.

**Head:** Medium-size
pure copper
bead.

**Thread:** Black UNI-
Thread.

**Tail:** Dyed black full marabou plume without stiff centre quill,
tied long.

**Body:** Crosscut strip of dyed black rabbit fur wound around the
shank.

## Palmered Brown Bug
*(Rory E. Glennie)*
For summer-run steelhead.

**Hook:** Mustad 94842, no. 12–8.
**Thread:** Black UNI-Thread.
**Tail:** Mixed grey and red fox squirrel tail hair.
**Rib:** 2–pound test monofilament counter-wound through hackle.
**Hackle:** Reddish brown saddle palmered heavily over the body.
**Body:** Even layer of tying thread.
**Wings:** As for tail, divided in two upright portions facing forward.
**Final step:** Clip bottom portion in an inverted V shape.

## Snootli
*(Rory E. Glennie)*
For summer-run steelhead.

**Hook:** Mustad 9671, no. 14–8.
**Thread:** Black UNI-Thread.
**Wing/Snout:** Red fox or grey squirrel tail hair, butts aligned with hook point, tips extending beyond the eye for at least one body length. Tie in behind eye, wrap tightly back to the butts, tie in hackle tip and wrap thread forward again.
**Hackle:** Natural red neck hackle for red fox squirrel, grizzly for grey squirrel, palmered heavily forward and tied off.

*Many fly fishers consider summer-run steelhead to be the ultimate challenge in Vancouver Island's rivers.*

Parksville resident **Rory E. Glennie** started tying flies in 1962 at age 10. Since moving from Ontario to BC in 1970, he has developed several popular West Coast freshwater and saltwater patterns. His articles appear in various outdoor magazines and he is West Coast field editor of *The Canadian Fly Fisher magazine.*

# CHAPTER SIX

*During migrations, feeding salmon can turn up on any beach, anywhere, at any time. As they draw closer to spawning, however, it pays to concentrate your fly fishing closer to the estuaries and nearby beaches.*

# FISHING THE
# NORTHERN FLATS *by Frank Dalziel*

Oh ne sunny August morning, while my brother Larry and I were wading along a sand flat seeking salmon, it occurred to me that we really do live in paradise. Like many fly fishers, I purchase magazines and dream of fishing faraway warm places for exotic saltwater species. You know, the grass is always greener … But as we waded the cold, clear water, I felt warm air and observed beautiful sand beaches with patches of eelgrass, gravel bars, large boulders, and sand dollar beds near estuaries, all of which were teeming with a great variety of sea life.

In my daydream we could have been in the tropics stalking bonefish; in reality we were in the Strait of Georgia's sheltered waters on the east coast of Vancouver Island, watching salmon schools finning in shallow water as the tide started flooding and the current increased.

*This wild coho is what beach fishing is all about.*

*The author probing the shallow northern flats on the Strait of Georgia.*

Larry cast up-tide, mended his line and dead-drifted his fly through a nearby school of fish in the shallows. His line paused and he tightened into a bright-silver coho salmon. It fought well, as coho do, but Larry soon led it beside his knee, then reached down to remove the barbless hook.

Welcome to the northeastern flats of the Pacific Ocean, seasonal home to many fish species pursued by fly fishers. With the exception of sockeye, all species of Pacific salmon can be fished in shallow water, but I will concentrate here on the tackle, flies, and tactics needed to fish for pink and coho salmon, which are most popular with fly fishers. They are common in shallow water and take flies readily—a great combination.

## TACKLE

Because saltwater is corrosive, purchase the best tackle you can afford. High-end rods and reels are not necessary, but should be designed and constructed to withstand the rigours of saltwater fishing. One outfit in the 6– to 8–weight range will suffice for both species.

*A saltwater fly reel should have a dependable drag system, ample line capacity and a corrosion resistant finish.*

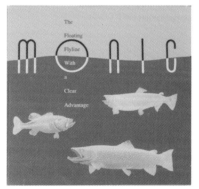

*For most beach fly fishing situations, a good quality floating line will be your best choice.*

Many excellent reels in the 6– to 8–weight range are designed for light saltwater use. I prefer large arbour models that recover line quickly and hold 200 yards of 20–pound test backing under the fly line. Though unnecessary for pinks, that capacity is comforting when a large coho runs toward open water—even more so if an occasional chinook happens by and inhales your fly.

My rod preference is a fast-action 6–weight, 9–foot 9–inch G.Loomis GL3; custom-made with a saltwater reel seat, oversize guides, and a detachable fighting butt. For coho, some use 7– or 8–weight rods, since heavier lines are easier to cast in wind and the fish average somewhat larger than pinks. I have tried these, but prefer my 6–weight because it is light and easier on my wrist. Most 9– to 10–foot rods with the characteristics mentioned are suitable.

While wading, I seldom fish in water deeper than 10 feet, so a floating line is all I recommend. I particularly like Monic clear floating line, which has virtually no memory in cold water. With it, flies can be presented to salmon milling in shallow or deep water, and it works well with fast to slow retrieves and dead-drifts (cast up-tide with no retrieve, even in the shallows. For maximum casting distance and top performance, lines should always be cleaned after fishing.

It is easier to approach salmon in shallow water that is covered by ripples or waves, and they are more often inclined to bite. Careless casting on calm days spooks salmon in shallow water. Long leaders, careful casting, and slow, cautious wading will help you hook fish under these tough conditions.

Premium leader material is essential for success. Tapered leaders 10 to 18 feet long are necessary on calm days, but in windy conditions, seven to nine feet is fine. I prefer fluorocarbon tippets of 12–pound test for pinks or coho, but many others use 6– to 12–pound test nylon monofilament.

*Always use premium grade nylon and fluorocarbon monofilament for your leaders and tippets.*

Use a Non-Slip Mono Loop Knot to connect the fly. It is strong and the fly tracks properly and moves freely. *Practical Fishing Knots* by Mark Sosin and Lefty Kreh (Lyons & Burfor Publishers) illustrates how to tie this and other useful knots like the surgeon's knot and the perfection loop knot.

Standard knots for connecting backing and leaders do not work on clear mono-core fly lines, so I use braided loops for all connections.

To learn how to make these, visit http://www.danblanton.com/gettinglooped.html.

# NON-SLIP MONO LOOP KNOT

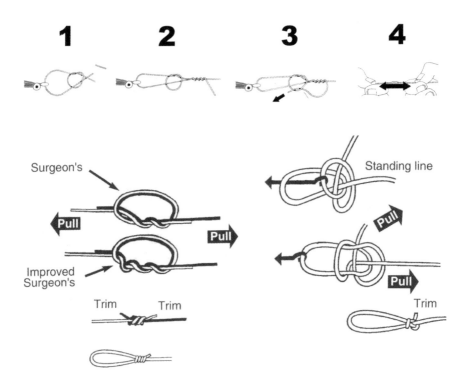

# MISCELLANEOUS GEAR

Essentials include a hat, polarized sunglasses, raincoat, chest waders, fly box, one or two spools of tippet material, spare leader, clippers, knife, hook hone, sun screen, and a haemostat or pliers. For safety, wear a wading belt to stop water from filling your waders in case of a fall.

When fishing for salmon on hot days, light, long-sleeved, vented shirts and breathable Gore-Tex waders are advisable. This gear wicks moisture and heat away from your body, making fishing more comfortable and enjoyable. Later in the season, layers of Polar Fleece clothing may be needed under Gore-Tex waders. Neoprene waders are an alternative in cool weather.

*Proper clothing attire and accessories can make or break a good fishing excursion. Choose these carefully and they will serve you for many years.*

# FISHING FOR PINK & COHO SALMON

*Dan Siminiuk casting for pinks at San Pariel Beach near Parksville.*

Fishing techniques for shallow-water pinks and coho are surprisingly similar. The ability to locate them makes knowledge of habitat, tides, beach topography and run timing essential. If new to the game, try to fish with someone who is experienced—and pay very close attention to everything that transpires.

Salmon have seasonal peaks in abundance that varies from area to area and year to year. The peak month for pinks is August, and for coho normally September or October.

Pinks are small fish (4 to 8 pounds), which start moving into shallow beach areas in Central and South Island waters some time during July (a couple of weeks earlier off North Island beaches near Port Hardy). Larger coho (5 to 15 pounds) follow in August or September, depending on location. Although seldom numerous, early pinks are in prime condition and may still be feeding. During migrations, feeding salmon can turn up on any beach, anywhere, at any time. When approaching their natal stream, large schools of pinks hold in shallow estuaries or adjacent bays until fall rains trigger their upstream exodus. Coho exhibit similar behaviour, but wander over larger areas and appear in smaller schools, offering great sport to those able to find them.

Some areas always hold fish, while others produce only occasionally, not necessarily every year (I wish I knew why). Vancouver Island has hundreds of miles of shoreline where fish move, hold, and feed in areas that see few anglers, so it pays to look around.

*Although the hump has started forming on this pink salmon, it is still bright. It fell for a Hakai Thorn.*

Once salmon are located, study where they are holding. Try examining the area at low tide to determine why fish hold there. Sometimes only a shallow depression in the bottom is found. Perhaps eelgrass or other weed beds, gravel, boulders, or sand dollar beds provide a dark background, making the salmon harder to see in the shallows. These habitats seem to attract fish whether the water depth is two feet or fifteen. Uneven sand or gravel bottoms with high and low spots are usually more productive than those that are flat and featureless.

Gravel points on beaches are great places from which to look for salmon, since they occasionally show their fins on the surface or move the water while swimming by. In any area fished, observant fly fishers watch for patterns of fish movements as they relate to time, location, and height of tide.

Pay attention to tides. Some areas fish well only on ebbs, others on floods, and some on both tides. Salmon move with the tides. It might only be 100 yards to the other side of a point or shoal, but this

*The author keeps his rod tip down while retrieving.*

knowledge can mean the difference between catching fish or getting skunked.

The right retrieve is often critical. One morning, while almost everyone was catching pinks, a fellow beside me remained fishless. He accepted a Pink Shrimp pattern from me, and I demonstrated the slow, one-foot strip retrieve I was using to hook fish. I even hooked one during the demonstration. Later, after releasing that fish, I glanced over and he was retrieving the fly like one might for coho, very fast. He was still fishless and extremely frustrated. After another demonstration, he managed to slow the fly down to the recommended long strip, pause, long strip, pause... By the time the flurry of activity ended he had landed six fish and was quite pleased with the outcome. He told me that no one had ever before suggested to him that he slow down. So bear in mind that some type of slow retrieve is usually the secret for pinks, and always worth trying for coho.

Other effective retrieves are short strips with pauses (vary the speed) and a "zooplankton retrieve," first described in *Flyfishing for Pacific Salmon* by Ferguson, Johnson, and Trotter (Frank Amato Publications). It's a 12–inch strip immediately followed by a quick, short downward flick of the wrist, "just like shaking down a thermometer," followed by a pause, then repeated. It works well. This book is still in print, and though dated in sections there is plenty of valuable information on flies, and fly fishing for Pacific salmon.

*Dalziel's Pink Shrimp.*

When salmon are really aggressive, stripping in the fly as fast as possible produces solid strikes. Otherwise, it is often ignored. Salmon swim faster than you can retrieve (after all, they catch bucktails and streamers trolled on the surface at extremely high speeds). When aggressively feeding, those fish will climb your arm to get into your fly box if you keep it open for too long, yet sometimes a fly dead-drifted with the tide works well. Always experiment with retrieves.

Good fly fishers catch fish because they move around, during which they remain technically sound, observant, and persistent. The best way to learn to fish is to do so almost every day, trying different retrieves and flies. Included here are dressings for six of my favourite flies for salmon on the shallow northern flats.

*Author releasing a wild coho that was hooked in knee-deep water on a shallow gravel flat.*

# SALT WATER FLY PATTERNS

### Blue And Green Bucktail
*(Larry Dalziel)*

Hook:    Daiichi 2546 or Tiemco 9394, no. 8–4

Thread:    Clear monofilament, fine or ultra-fine

Belly:    White polar bear hair, sparse

Wing:    Stacked chartreuse polar bear hair, sparse, 4 Strands chartreuse Krystal Flash, sparse silver doctor blue polar bear topped with 6–8 strands of blue Krystal Flash.

Lateral line: 1 strand pearl Flashabou tied on each side

Head:    Build up thread

Eyes:    1.5 mm silver or pearl adhesive Mylar

Gills:    6/0 fluorescent red thread wrapped in a thin band behind head.

Finish:    5–minute epoxy over head. Rotate fly until epoxy sets.

### Larry's Fly
*(Larry Dalziel)*

Hook:    Daiichi 2546 (heavy), Mustad C 47S (medium), or Mustad C 49S (light), no. 8–6

Thread:    6/0 fluorescent chartreuse

Tail:    6–8 strands olive Krystal Flash, body length

Body:    Pearl Diamond Braid, olive

Throat:    6–8 strands of olive Krystal Flash

Comments: To increase sink rate or to add a bit of flash, add silver beads of 3/32–, 1/8– or 5/32–inch diameter.

**Pink Shrimp**
*(modified from John
O'Brien original)*
*Frank Dalziel*

**Hook:** Daiichi 2456, no. 8–6.
**Thread:** 6/0 fluorescent red.
**Tail:** Bubble gum pink polar
bear.
**Eyes:** Optional. Small olive Mono Nymph Eye.
**Body:** Fluorescent fuchsia wool or 4–strand floss.
**Shellback:** 12 strands of KF02 (Fluorescent Cerise) Krystal Flash
**Rib:** Fluorescent red 6/0 thread binding Krystal Flash to body
**Finish:** Light coat of Krazy Glue on Krystal Flash for durability.


**Coho Bugger**
*(modified from Bob Weir original)*
*Frank Dalziel*

**Hook:** Daiichi 2546, no.
4–6 (or size and model of
choice).
**Thread:** 6/0 fluorescent chartreuse.
**Tail:** Chartreuse polar bear, sparse (hook length or slightly
shorter), topped with 4 strands chartreuse Krystal Flash
**Rib:** Green wire, counter-wound.
**Hackle:** 5–6 turns of no. 2 grizzly saddle (slightly longer than hook
gap).
**Body:** Pearl Diamond Braid dyed fluorescent chartreuse.

**Cathy's Coat**
*(My version of a Bob Weir/Barry Thornton favourite)*
*Frank Dalziel*

**Hook:** TMC 9394, no. 10–4.
**Thread:** 6/0 fluorescent red.
**Body:** Fluorescent red floss or steelhead yarn, wrapped flat and thin.
**Wing:** White polar bear, sparse, to end of shank.
**Topping:** 10–12 strands of pearl Flashabou.

**Pink Candy**
*(Art Limber)*
**Hook:** Tiemco 9394, no. 10–8
**Thread:** 6/0 fluorescent red.
**Tail:** Fluorescent pink hackle fibres.
**Body:** 12 strands rainbow Krystal Flash wound around shank.
**Back:** Fluorescent pink hackle fibres tied down at rear.
**Head:** Build up of tying thread.
**Eyes:** 1.5 mm red adhesive Mylar.
**Body coat:** 5–minute epoxy. Rotate fly until epoxy sets.

*Clouser Minnows, Coho Buggers and Candy Flies make up the bulk of Frank Dalziel's ready-use fly box.*

*A typical hatchery coho hooked over a cobblestone bottom similar to the background. The author was using a 6–weight rod, floating line and a Coho Bugger. Also displayed is a boxful of patterns that attract shallow-water salmon throughout the season. Note the predominance of pink and chartreuse.*

*Author Frank Dalziel releasing a small hatchery coho. The protective "gloves" on his right thumb and index finger prevent painful line cuts.*

Lantzville resident **Frank Dalziel** tied his first fly before he was 10, and has keenly studied fly tying in the 40 years since. A former salt-water fishing guide, he is now a Fisheries Technologist at Malaspina University-College, where he shares his lifelong fascination for fish, bugs, fishing, and fish habitats.

# CHAPTER SEVEN

*An average-sized smallmouth from Shawnigan Lake.*

# SOUTH ISLAND SMALLMOUTH BONANZA *by Bill Luscombe*

While preparing to teach a fly-casting class several years ago, one of my students related a tale about the great fly fishing for smallmouth bass found in some lakes on southern Vancouver Island. I spoke with my informant for quite awhile, during which time others joined in on the conversation. As it turned out, there were more than a few people familiar with the fly fishing opportunities for smallmouths on the Island.

I was fascinated and quite excited about "discovering" a new fishery (at least new to me), but knowing very little about bass at the time, I decided to research as much as possible about these fish and their habits before venturing out in pursuit of them.

Off I went to the library, and also spent time searching through the Internet. I turned up a great deal of information, and found it quite interesting to learn about the life cycle and spawning habits of smallmouth bass, as well as the different tactics that can be used to catch them. Some of the more interesting things I discovered were:

- Smallmouth bass are not members of the bass family at all, but of the sunfish family. Their Latin name is *Micropterus dolomieui*.
- They lack an adipose fin, but have two dorsal fins that are joined, and the first one contains 10 sharp spines. They look very much like

*Smallmouths have two dorsal fins. The front one contains sharp spines. They have no adipose fin.*

*The eyes of smallmouth bass are usually red or orange.*

a saltwater rockfish, especially the sporty black rockfish (a favourite with fly fishers).

- Their colouring in stained water is very dark, and they aren't very attractive when found in tea-coloured lakes. In clear lakes, however, they take on their more natural green and gold colouring, and are actually quite pretty. You can easily distinguish a smallmouth from a large mouth by the former's red eyes.

- Bass spawn annually around the last week of May, and can do so in still water as well as moving water. I found this interesting, since trout and salmon need moving water to successfully spawn because their eggs require ongoing oxygenation.

- They usually set up spawning "nests" on sand, gravel or rocky bottoms within 150 metres of their previous year's nest. This was also interesting, as it indicated that they must spend their lives close to where they were born, and thus are probably territorial.

- The male smallmouth builds the nest, usually in water depths ranging from one to six feet, but occasionally deeper. When finished, the concave nest is a circular patch of sand and gravel about twice the diameter of the male's length, in the centre of which are clustered some larger stones.

- Up to three females may take part in populating a nest. Once spawning is complete, the female departs and the male remains to guard the nest. His protective role is complicated by hordes of small predatory fish, which are intent on eating his progeny. For each predator that is chased away, several others dart in to steal eggs. This non-stop process often ends with 80 per cent or more of the eggs eaten before hatching occurs.

- The tiny black fry remain over the nest for five to seven days before starting to venture briefly away from it. Predation increases accordingly, although the male continues guarding his brood for several days while these exploratory excursions continue.

- Conservation-minded anglers never fish for bedding bass, even if they intend to release them, for removing a protective male from his nest exposes the eggs and small hatchlings to heavy predation.

- Smallmouths have a lifespan of about 16 years and reach maturity at age four. They can attain a length of up to 27 inches (69 cm). (Wow!)

- Bass are most active in temperatures between 16° and 24° Celsius (60° and 75° Fahrenheit). This was another great discovery, for it meant I could keep fishing into the heat of summer, when trout stop feeding and sulk on the bottom, and for fish that remain active and still fight well in warm water.

- Smallmouths are opportunistic predators that eat almost anything, but prefer crayfish and larger morsels like small frogs, sculpins and minnows. Good information to remember when tying flies for bass.

- They stay near bottom and stick to structure like downed trees, wharf pilings and docks, where they can hide in the shadows and dart out to attack unsuspecting passers by.

They are quite tasty and there are lots of excellent recipes for cooking bass. This was great news, too, because I love to eat fish. And so, after doing all of this research it was time to do some live field-testing by

*Smallmouths like shoreline structure that provides safety and concealment.*

goin' fishin' for bass. I cornered my buddy, Clive, and we decided to venture to St. Mary Lake on Saltspring Island to check things out.

St. Mary is a large lake that is stocked with rainbow/steelhead and cutthroats; however, it also supports a thriving population of small-mouth bass—which was what we were after.

After a quick breakfast we caught an early ferry from Crofton to Vesuvius on Saltspring, which is only a few minutes drive from the lake. The morning was a bit cloudy and breezy when we parked at the little beach on the lake's north end. Lily pads bordered the lakeshore, and we could see a small island about 400 yards offshore. We readied our

*Clive Baudin with a fairly typical smallmouth bass that was caught and released at St. Mary Lake on Saltspring Island.*

tackle, launched our float tubes, and were soon finning along the edges of the lily pads. Rather than play leapfrog with each other, I decided to head out to the island and give that area a try, leaving Clive behind to continue working the shoreline.

By the time I arrived at the island the wind was kicking up a bit, but not quite whitecapping. Casting from deeper water in toward the shallows near the island, I drew my fly slowly back over what I could plainly see was a rock-strewn bottom. Before retrieving it halfway back, a 13-inch smallmouth snapped it up. It fought very much like a brook trout—bulldogging, trying to keep its nose down and return to deeper water, while I tried my best to keep it from doing just that.

I quickly landed the chunky fish, admired it briefly, then released it. I cast to the same spot again, and once more my fly was struck after just a few strips. I landed and released that bass as well, then yelled at Clive to come over and get in on the fun.

It took Clive about 15 minutes to fin-kick his way over to the island, and by the time he arrived I had landed about a dozen bass, all in the 13- to 18-inch range. It had been virtually a bass a cast.

We continued fishing for the rest of the morning, and must have each hooked into 40 or more bass in slightly less than three hours. With afternoon getting on and the wind picking up badly, we decided that we'd had enough and headed for home. Our arms were getting tired, anyway—always a good sign of a great day's fishing.

Clive and I had found out from our little adventure that smallmouth bass are a great game fish-feisty, tough, spunky roughnecks that jump, cartwheel and tailwalk on the surface. We agreed that they reminded us of football linebackers, and were certainly worthy of further pursuit.

Since that first trip to St. Mary Lake I have fished for smallmouths every spring, both on Vancouver Island and Saltspring Island. They have provided many days of productive, enjoyable fly fishing, and given me valuable insight into this species. I now look forward to angling for these little scrappers every year.

*Shawnigan Lake yields some fair-sized smallmouth bass like this one Clive Baudin is leading to net.*

# WHERE TO GO

There are quite a few lakes on southern Vancouver Island that hold good-sized smallmouth bass, and about 17 are accessible to the public. In and around Victoria are Elk, Beaver, Langford, and Glen lakes, as well as Matheson and Young lakes near Sooke. All offer good populations of smallmouths. North toward Duncan, Shawnigan Lake has some large bass. I have caught them up to four pounds there—and lost one that would have gone heavier.

On Saltspring Island, Cusheon, Stowell, and St. Mary lakes hold fair-sized bass, and the latter is well known for its large population of smallmouths.

*While fly fishing for bass, Ian Forbes prefers the comfort and higher seating provided by a pontoon boat to that of a float tube.*

*The many bays branching out from the main body of Quennell Lake offer opportunities for smallmouth bass, rainbows and cutthroat trout.*

Chemainus and Fuller lakes near Chemainus offer smaller-sized bass. Although I have caught a number of them there, I have yet to hook into anything over a pound. Farther north, Quennell Lake near Nanaimo is a very popular spot to fish for smallmouths that grow to four pounds and heavier. Other Nanaimo area lakes with bass include Long, Green, Diver and Holden. Spider Lake, almost due west of Qualicum Beach, holds smallmouths that also get to a fair size. It is the northern-most lake on the Island with bass.

*Susan Luscombe had her hands full with this Shawnigan Lake smallmouth, but slow and easy won the day.*

# EQUIPMENT

Fly tackle for smallmouths need not be any different from what you normally use for trout. A 4– or 5–weight system works great, but the lighter tackle is more fun.

A small capacity reel with a standard pawl-drag will work just fine. Bass do not make long runs, so you need not worry about having a lot of backing at your disposal. A floating line will get you through most situations, but a sink-tip might come in handy at times, and even a slow-sink has its place. Smallmouths aren't leader shy, so a standard 9–foot tapered leader will do quite nicely.

*A large Shawnigan Lake smallmouth gave Clive Baudin's tackle a good work-out before it was finally released.*

# FLY PATTERNS & TECHNIQUES FOR USING THEM

Fly fishing for smallmouth bass is easy. Because of their affinity for cover, you need simply locate obvious spots and get your fly to them, often down near the bottom. Casting is the only way to do this; trolling flies for bass doesn't work well at all. Some of the best places to locate fish are under and around boat docks and wharfs, and areas with rocky outcrops that drop off quickly into deeper water. I have had very good luck in all such situations.

The best wet patterns are those that offer big bites and show lots of motion. Marabou flies like a Yellow-Bellied Woolly Bugger and Forbes' Shaggy Dragon in size 10 or 8 work exceptionally well, as do various Woolly Worms, Marabou Muddlers and leech patterns. Flies with a bit of gaudy colour seem to attract the attention of bass better than the bland olives and blacks of standard trout ties, so try adding a bit of colour to your trout patterns.

I find that a short-strip retrieve interspersed with slow hand-twists every so often works well. Vary the speed of your retrieve to give the fly material an undulating motion as it swims through the water. It's sort of like strutting down in the bad part of town and thumbing your nose at the hoods—those thug-like bass are just bound to attack sooner or later.

*A Black Woolly Bugger is a good leech imitation for bass.*

Many anglers like catching bass on dry flies. Trout patterns like the Madam-X, Tom Thumb, and Mikulak Sedge work well in larger sizes, as do simple spun deer hair "bugs." The ticket is to cast to a likely spot, then simply let the fly sit there, unmoving, for 30 seconds or more. Then give it just the slightest twitch. If a smallmouth has been watching it intently, which they often do, it will go ballistic and make a noisy surface grab or, most spectacular of all, leap out of the water and grab the fly while going back down.

Fishing for smallmouth bass on the South Island is rapidly becoming a "second season" for trout anglers, and while fly fishing for them is still relatively new, it is catching on quickly. This is no surprise to me. The hot days of summer are great times to be on the water, and a few active bass make them even better—so get out and hook into a few. Consider it your civic duty, then if anyone asks what you're doing, just tell them you're trying to take back the neighbourhood from the thugs and ruffians.

# FAVOURITE BASS PATTERNS

## Shaggy Dragon
*(Ian Forbes)*

**Hook:** Mustad 9671, no. 8–6.

**Thread:** Olive.

**Eyes:** Closed cell foam dumb-bells for patterns designed to float above bottom while remaining relatively motionless; metal or plastic dumb-bells or Bead Chain for sinking patterns.

**Tail:** Plymouth Rock soft body feather dyed orange-brown.

**Underbody:** Use a closed cell foam strip on floating Dragons, nothing on sinkers.

**Body:** Clumps of Plymouth Rock soft body feather dyed orange-brown.

**Hackle:** Speckled Guinea fowl dyed orange brown.


## Yellow Marabou Muddler
*(Dave Whitlock) Robert H. Jones*

**Hook:** Mustad 79580, no. 10–6.

**Tail:** Red hackle fibres.

**Body:** Silver Diamond Braid.

**Wing:** Yellow marabou over yellow calf tail or bucktail (or colours of choice).

**Topping:** Peacock herl.

**Collar/Head:** Deer or caribou hair, spun and clipped bullet shape. Leave a fringe untrimmed for collar.

### Yellow-Bellied Woolly Bugger
*(Russell Blessing) Robert H. Jones*

| | |
|---|---|
| **Hook:** | Mustad 79580, no. 10–6. |
| **Thread:** | 6/0 red UNI-Thread. |
| **Tail:** | Yellow marabou. |
| **Hackle:** | Red, palmered through body. |
| **Rib:** | Fine silver or gold wire, counterwound ovehackle. |
| **Body:** | Yellow chenille. |

### Fast Madam X
*(Bob Jones variation of Doug Swisher's original)*

| | |
|---|---|
| **NOTE:** | This version eliminates the tail of deer hair and calls for a bullet-shaped head (Thunder Creek style). |
| **Hook:** | Mustad 79580, no. 10–6. |
| **Thread:** | Kevlar, colour of choice. |
| **Body:** | Thread. |
| **Legs:** | Two 1–inch lengths of white, fine diameter rubber strand or Lycra. |
| **Wing:** | Deer hair. Tie in butts with tips facing forward, wind thread rearward about ⅜–inch. Fold hair rearward and bind to shank forming a narrow waist. Cut the hair across the bottom just behind the waist and trim as necessary to expose body. Tie in a rubber strand on each side. Tie off and trim strands so rear legs are slightly longer than front legs. |

*When summer doldrums put the trout down deep, find a smallmouth bass lake and get aquainted with these truly great game fish.*

*Author Bill Luscombe quickly learned to appreciate the strength and acrobatic abilities of smallmouth bass.*

A Professional Forester for the Provincial Government, Crofton resident **Bill Luscombe** started fly fishing and tying his own flies in 1981. A prolific writer whose articles appear in various outdoor magazines, he also teaches courses on fishing and hunting.

*Originally stocked in selected Vancouver Island waters during the 1930s, brown trout provide an exciting challenge for fly fishers.*

# BROWN TROUT ON
# VANCOUVER ISLAND *by Ian Forbes*

B rown trout were originally stocked on Vancouver Island during the 1930s, but only in Cameron Lake and the Cowichan River have these European imports naturalized into a self-sustaining population.

*The Cowichan River is noted for its healthy population of brown trout.*

Although large browns are caught occasionally in Cameron Lake, they have never provided a good fly fishery. Most are taken by trolling, and it yields fish in double-digit weights, including a very impressive trophy of 19 pounds 2 ounces in 2004.

A few browns also trickled downstream into the Little Qualicum River, and while occasional fish are still encountered they have never established a firm foothold. It is an entirely different story in the Cowichan River, which has proved to be ideal habitat. They have established a solid niche in this system, and the Cowichan has long been the most popular river in British Columbia for anglers who want to catch a brown trout.

In the 1980s and 1990s, browns were stocked in other lakes and streams on Vancouver Island. Lois Lake, Tadjiss Lake, McClure Lake, Rooney Lake, and the upper Adam River all received several plantings. Both Lois and Tadjiss lakes are in the private Shawnigan Division logging area south of Duncan, where access is restricted to weekends only. Outlet streams from these lakes flow into Holt Creek, which in turn flows into the Cowichan River. McClure Lake is in an entirely different watershed in the headwaters of the Caycuse River, where access is restricted to after logging hours. North of Campbell River, Rooney Lake is in the Adam River watershed, and the Adam River is a tributary to the Eve River. The Island highway crosses the upper Adam River and provides what little access is available.

Lois Lake proved to be ideal habitat where browns grew quickly to well over 20 inches. Dragonflies and damselflies are abundant in this

*Float tubes are excellent modes of transportation on smaller lakes with brown trout.*

reed-lined lake, and the stocked trout grew fat on them. However, landing those big trout was another story, for most of them broke the angler's leaders on the reeds. It remained a popular fishery for several years but, unfortunately, the spawning stream was unable to maintain their numbers and the large browns slowly died off. With no further plantings there are now very few browns remaining in Lois Lake. Only hatchery cutthroats and rainbows are currently stocked, and none grow to the size of those early brown trout.

Tadjiss Lake does not produce as much trout food as Lois Lake and had only marginal success with stocked browns, which seemed to die off about the same time as those in Lois Lake. In McClure Lake, all of the brown trout fry seemed to vanish right after planting, but in the early 2000s an angler fishing bait caught a 17–pounder. Whether any other browns remain in that system remains a mystery.

Browns didn't appear to establish a breeding population in tiny Rooney Lake either, but an experiment with nutrient enhancement in the upper Adam River saw browns stocked there do quite well.

*Author Ian Forbes with a prime Adam River brown trout. Nutrient enhancement created a viable brown trout fishery in this North Island stream, and a few are also present in nearby Rooney Lake.*

Unfortunately, that program was dropped due to lack of government funding. As recently as 2001 there were still a few browns available in the Adam River, and while they appear to have scattered throughout the system, without continued upper stream nutrient enhancement a reliable food source is lacking.

Browns appear able to withstand slightly higher water temperatures than rainbow or cutthroat trout. This has allowed them to adjust to warm summer water in the Cowichan River and remain in residence, rather than migrate back into the lake like the rainbows. They also live longer and survive after spawning, which might explain their larger size in mixed species environments. There is no question that most of the trout over 20 inches caught in the Cowichan will be browns rather than the more abundant rainbows.

Brown trout are far more predatory than rainbows, which puts them about on a par with cutthroats. Rainbows feed primarily on insects until they are at least 16 inches long. As soon as they reach eight or nine

*Large browns like meat in their diet, which means they target small fish whenever the opportunity presents itself.*

inches, both browns and cutthroats start preying on minnows, and by the time a brown is 12 inches long it will actively search for and feed on salmon fry to the exclusion of other food items. Upon reaching 20 inches, they will eat young steelhead smolts over six inches long. Very large browns become predators almost exclusively, and can easily gulp down a 12–inch trout. This is why river keepers in the UK and Europe will usually cull these big bruisers from the breeding or rearing pools of their closely manicured systems. They will, however, leave them in the main river to prey on weak or sick fish, which also provides anglers with an opportunity to try for the trophy-sized trout.

*Evening low light periods are when large browns really turn on to feeding, and this continues after darkness.*

Notorious for being low light feeders, browns do most of their dining during the evening, after dark and all night, right into early morning twilight. This is especially the case after the main insect hatches have finished in the spring, and be warned that it's seldom productive to fish for them before 7 p.m. during the summer months.

Being fall spawners, from November through early December browns will be found in specific sections of rivers called "staging areas." At this time the big males are especially vulnerable due to their aggressive behaviour, and will smash any large Woolly Bugger or similar streamer pattern that comes near them. Other than catch-and-release regulations there is no protection for browns at this time, but ethical anglers will leave them alone.

During heavy insect hatches, browns lose a little of their native caution and feed selectively on whatever is hatching; however, they can be particularly fussy about patterns and presentation. They are less likely to be selective when there is not a hatch, but remain much more aware of their surroundings. A steadily feeding trout can be approached quite closely, but that same trout just resting in the shallows will spook at the first sign of an intruder.

*Large patterns like a Woolly Worm or this Mink Hair Leech often trigger strikes from moody browns.*

The meadow area of the Little Qualicum River makes a nice walk-and-wade fishery, but cutthroat trout are far more common there than browns. The best section is closed during the spring and summer, with the only open area a short section below Cameron Lake.

As mentioned earlier, Cameron Lake produces occasional trophy browns for anglers who troll with plugs, but success usually takes many hours of patience and persistence. Rapala plugs seem to be the most popular lure by far, but trolling a streamer or minnow-imitating pattern also attracts attention now and then. The shoal at the mouth of

*Ian Forbes leads a brown to net on the Little Qualicum River.*

*A sculpin imitation like this Golden Muddler Minnow provides a real mouthful for a marauding brown trout.*

the Cameron River is a good area to begin, but don't hesitate to explore, for the browns might be anywhere.

This leaves the Cowichan River as being the most consistent producer of brown trout in British Columbia. Most are caught in the upper river, above Skutz Falls in the "block 51 area," or between the old 70.2–mile railway bridge and the village of Lake Cowichan. An

*The Cowichan is British Columbia's premier brown trout river.*

occasional brown is taken farther downstream in the Stoltz Park area, but they are far less common, and they are seldom taken in the lower river at all.

Depending on where and when you fish will determine the most productive method and fly pattern to employ. From October through early spring the most consistent pattern is a Single Egg Fly. A pale, peach pink pattern with a touch of orange is deadly, but it must be rolled naturally along the bottom below where salmon are spawning. Every good pool below a gravel spawning area will have trout feeding on the excess salmon eggs washing downstream.

Streamers, bucktails, Muddler Minnows and Woolly Buggers are always good choices for brown trout. The most common salmon fry in the Cowichan are chums, coho and Chinooks. Chum fry head to the ocean in March and are gone within a week. Chinook fry stay around a bit longer, but are usually heading for the ocean by April. Coho fry

*During the salmon spawning period it is wise to use egg patterns to tempt brown trout.*

*The proof is in the catching—an egg imitation drifted behind spawning salmon yielded this fine brown trout.*

stay in the river for a year, locating in all of the back eddies and slow sections. This leaves coho fry as the most important prey species for brown trout. When the little fry start feeding on midges in the evening, the browns stalk them along the willows. Anywhere that willow trees have taken root in the river will have holding water nearby.

The Cowichan has a good insect population in the upper river. Turn over any boulder and nymphs will be seen clinging to the underside or trying to escape. Golden stoneflies are the first important insect to hatch, and those big nymphs crawl to shore prior to emerging. Trout will take the free-crawling nymphs along the bottom and later slurp

*Rob Brown's Summer Muddler is a good "go to" pattern after the spawning season dies off.*

*Juvenile coho remain in a river for a year, making them an important food item for brown trout. A Forbes Floating Minnow is an excellent imitation.*

the egg-laying adults floating in the surface film.

Small to medium-size browns will feed on golden stoneflies in late March and early April, and on mayflies and the little brown caddis during April and May. When western march brown mayflies hatch in early April, all of the trout will be there to greet them, including browns, rainbows and occasional cutthroats. If the water is too high, the trout will take nymphs in preference to adults on the surface.

During sunny weather in early May, the western march brown spinners will do their midday dance, which usually brings trout to the surface. After the first hot spell in mid to late May, there is usually a

*Cowichan browns also feed heavily on aquatic insects at times, so don't overlook patterns that imitate them.*

flight of big, black carpenter ants. Trout will feed exclusively on them for about one day before going off their feed for the following four or five days while they digest the ants.

In late May and early June, the Cowichan River usually drops and starts warming up, and most of the larger rainbows and cutthroats migrate back to the lake. A few browns also head for the lake, while others seek a few spring-fed pools farther downstream. Before the river gets too warm there can be good evening fisheries during what is called the "evening drift."

*A Golden Stone is a good pattern during March and early April.*

This is when insects drift freely in the current and repopulate the river downstream. When you can find them, the browns will take tiny mayfly patterns that must be delivered with a perfect drag-free drift. They will also take large minnow patterns, which must be swung downstream on a sinking line and then fished back along the willows.

After the first hot spell of summer elevates the water temperature, brown trout in the Cowichan River should be left alone until the water cools again.

*As water in the Cowichan warms during late May and early June, try evening float trips and concentrate on the deeper holes.*

The stress of playing a trout in warm water conditions might very well kill it, and such worthy opponents deserve much more respect.

# TROUT FLY PATTERNS

## Muddler Minnow

*(Don Gapen)*
*Mac Warner*

**Hook:** No. 2–12.
**Thread:** Black.
**Tail:** Brown turkey strip.
**Body:** Flat gold tinsel.
**Wing:** Brown turkey sections over grey squirrel tail extending to end of head.
**Head:** Natural brown deer hair, spun and clipped to shape, tapered toward hook eye.

## Floating Minnow

*(Ian Forbes)*

**Hook:** Mustad 9671, no. 4–8.
**Thread:** White, wrapped from eye to bend.
**Tail:** Brownish orange marabou.

**Underbody:** Silvery or white packing foam (found on electronics and wine bottles). Tie in at front and rear but do not compress. Daub 3 purple spots on each side.
**Body:** Large diameter braided pearl Mylar slid over the underbody and back, then tied in at hook eye.
**Epoxy:** Angler's Choice Soft Body to coat entire body.
**Eyes:** 2 mm adhesive Mylar added after body dries.
**Glue:** Bond 527. After body dries, coat the back with this fast-drying glue.
**Back:** Barred pintail or teal flank feather dyed dark olive. Place lengthwise down the back and press into position. When the glue has dried, add a second coat of Soft Body to the body.

**Egg Fly**
*(Brian Smith)*
**Hook:** Mustad 9174, no. 10–8.
**Thread:** Red UTC.
**Underbody:** 5–7 wraps of .020" lead wire,
starting 1/16" behind the eye.
**Body:** A finger-width clump of fire
orange Glo Yarn tied tightly on
top center of shank with figure–8 wraps, then another on
the bottom. Bring top ends together, pull upward and cut
as close to the shank as possible. Rotate hook and repeat on
the bottom. Trim to a ball shape.
**Veil:** A pencil-width clump of white Glo Yarn tied in front of
body and smoothed rearward around body, creating a sparse
veil. Trim ends slightly longer than the body.

**Western March
Brown Nymph**
*(Ian Forbes)*
**Hook:** Mustad 9671,
no. 14.
**Thread:** Olive.
**Tail:** Drake pintail
duck flank
feather fibres
dyed ginger.
**Rib:** Fine copper wire.
**Belly:** Dubbing: rear half mahogany brown, front half ginger.
**Legs:** Guinea fowl speckled body feather dyed ginger-brown.
**Wing pad:** Dark brown turkey coated twice with clear lacquer.
**Thorax:** Bronze peacock herl.

## Western March Brown Dun
*(Ian Forbes)*

**Hook:** Mustad 9671, no. 14.

**Thread:** Olive.

**Tail:** 4 strands of moose mane same length as hook. To make fly land hook point up, tail must be mounted partly around the bend.

**Body:** Ginger tan dubbing.

**Thorax:** Reddish brown dubbing.

**Wing:** Optional. A few strands of barred pintail flank feather.

**Hackle:** Grizzly dyed dun or dark sandy dun, forced to sides by bringing thorax dubbing forward and back over the belly in figure–8 wraps.

**Note:** As hook point is not submerged, this fly floats lightly on the surface and looks far more realistic from below.

## Little Brown Cowichan Caddis
*(Ian Forbes)*

**Hook:** Mustad 9671, no. 14, or 9484 no. 12.

**Thread:** Brown.

**Abdomen:** Medium brown dubbing with fine bits of olive Flashabou dubbing mixed in.

**Wing:** Dyed brown plastic string material or very thin plastic Raffia in transparent brown, as a thin veil over the body.

**Hackle:** Medium brown.

**Black Carpenter Ant**
*(Ian Forbes)*

**Hook:** Mustad 94840, no. 12.
**Thread:** Black Kevlar.
**Body:** Closed cell foam cylinder. Round ends with scissors, make a shallow slice to accommodate shank. Trim out a little foam where thread will compress it. Colour body and coat with nail polish before continuing.
**Wing:** Optional. Ginger hackle tips.
**Hackle:** 3 wraps of black neck hackle.
**Misc.:** Black marker pen, Sally Hansen Hard as Nails nail polish.

**Foam Body Golden Stone**
*(Ian Forbes)*

**Hook:** Mustad 9671, no. 10–8.
**Thread:** Olive or yellow.
**Tail:** Yellow goose biots.
**Body:** Strip of closed cell white foam wrapped around shank and coloured with yellow marker pen.
**Wing:** Plastic string material or thin plastic raffia coloured with brown marker pen.
**Hackle:** Light ginger or golden badger.
**Head:** Closed cell foam.

**Golden Stone
Nymph (BC)**
*(Phil Milburn)*

**Hook:** TMC 200R, no. 2-8.

**Thread:** 6/0 tan.

**Eyes:** 30–pound test brown nylon monofilament melted on ends.

**Tail:** Gold or brown goose biots. Dub a small ball at top of bend to separate the biots into a V-shape.

**Underbody:** Lead wire wrapped on shank and flattened.

**Abdomen:** Woven yellow and brown Larva Lace.

**Wingcase:** Brown turkey feather coated with Dave's Flexament.

**Thorax/Head:** Kaufman Golden Stone Dubbing, wound forward between the legs.

**Legs:** Gold or brown goose biots, bent by heating tweezers.

**Antennae:** Gold or brown goose biots.

**Final step:** Fold wingcase twice, then fold down in front of the head and tie in behind hook eye. Fold back over the head and tie in with a thread collar behind the front legs.

*Cameron Lake yields trophy-sized browns to those who put in the time. Larry E. Stefanyk took this one on a Black Leech.*

*Brown trout are a real success story in some Vancouver Island rivers and lakes.*

*Author Ian Forbes with an early-morning Cowichan River brown trout.*

A retired Forester, **Ian Forbes** has fished throughout British Columbia, the western provinces and USA, plus Asia, New Zealand, Australia, Central America and England. A well-known outdoor writer, he is also a freelance artist whose works have illustrated many books and hundreds of magazine articles, and his water colour paintings hang in several galleries and private collections.

# CHAPTER NINE

*Tim Tullis took this 17½–pound coho at Clayoquot Sound on his Tim's Olive Needlefish pattern.*

# OPEN-OCEAN FLY FISHING FOR COHO *by Tim Tullis*

If hearing a screaming reel and following the antics of a high-jumping, cartwheeling silver bullet creates that adrenalin rush so highly sought after by most fly fishers, give open ocean fly fishing for coho a try.

The thought of fly fishing water larger than a lake or river can be a little disconcerting to many anglers. It needn't be. Although we are all still in the beginning stages of understanding when it comes to any form of saltwater fly fishing, you should garner enough information in this chapter to get you going with some degree of confidence.

Coho are found from Alaska's Bering Sea to Monterey Bay in central California; however, we on Vancouver Island are privileged to have an abundance of water that lends itself to open ocean fly fishing. My preference is water 15 to 50 feet deep, which has good bottom structure and an abundance of kelp beds.

Although there are always a few resident coho scattered up and down the West Coast, the best fishing occurs when migrating runs are heading for their home waters. Mid-June usually marks the arrival of initial runs, which continue throughout September and even into October.

*Rocky outcrops and kelp beds provide structural cover for baitfish, which in turn attracts predatory salmon.*

# TACKLE

**Rods:** I recommend 8– to 10–weights of various lengths. My first choice is a 9–foot, 8–weight. An 8–weight nicely handles most fish hooked, and 9 feet is long enough to cast easily yet short enough to be easily stored while running between fishing spots. An 8–weight effectively handles fly lines to 300 grains, which covers about 80 percent of the fishing situations you will face.

I also recommend a backup rod. I carry a 9–foot, 10–weight for two reasons: in situations with fast-running tides, it allows the use of heavier lines or shooting heads to get down to the fish; and when Chinooks are in the area, it's comforting to have a more powerful rod handy.

*Dave Petryk on Clayoquot Sound with his first coho on a cast fly. The impressive 12½–pounder hit a Tim's Llama Needlefish.*

**Reels:** A matter of personal choice, but with some qualifiers:

- Choose one that will stand up to salt water use.
- It should have the capacity to hold a full 8–weight fly line and at least 200 yards of 30–pound test backing.
- A good, reliable drag system is a must.

*A fast-sinking line is usually a saltwater fly fisher's first choice.*

**Lines:** The majority of my fishing is done with an Airflo Depthfinder 300–grain line with a floating running line. In addition to a 7½ inch-per-second sink rate that gets your fly down in a hurry, it has exceptional casting qualities and should handle the majority of your fishing challenges. My second choice is a Rio Striper 26–foot Density Compensated VersiTip Coldwater Line, which comes with a variety of interchangeable tips ranging from intermediate to 450 grains. Additional tips can also be

*Fly lines should range from floating to extra-fast sinking, which makes shooting heads popular.*

added to your arsenal. My collection includes a floater and a variety of heads up to 850 grains.

If you have the reels, spare spools, and the capability to tote them along, you probably can't have too many lines. Often, a condition or event occurs when you discover that you haven't yet seen it all. For example, one evening while fishing off Wickaninnish Island with partner Gus Averill, the school of coho we were zeroed in on disappeared. Our lengthy search produced no results, so we decided to explore a group of rocks about 1.5 kilometers beyond the surf line.

Within seconds of arriving, we

*A floating line, a saltwater popper and a school of surface-feeding black rockfish is a guarantee of fast-paced fishing action.*

both had savage strikes that produced two very strong, 4– to 5–pound black rockfish. Fortunately, I had a floating line and a handful of salt-water poppers with me. We tied off to some nearby kelp and enjoyed an hour of hilarious fun fishing for black rockfish to 6 pounds. These fish aggressively attack a popper by jumping completely out of the water—often 2 or 3 at the same time—then inhale the bug on the way down. You are guaranteed to break into fits of laughter while involved with the comical antics of a school of large black rockfish. I should add that they are fantastic table fare, but suggest you keep only a couple, for they are very slow-growing fish.

**Leader:** At times coho seem to be leader shy, and at others they are reckless about pursuing a meal. My choice is fluorocarbon with a nylon tippet that is stiff and abrasion-resistant: stiff to carry the fly in windy conditions, and abrasion-resistant to reduce the number of cut leaders should a coho inhale the fly.

Manufactured tapered leaders are fine, but I prefer making my own with a butt section of about 18 inches of 25–pound test, an equal length of 20–pound test, and a 2–foot tippet of 15–pound test. Yes, I fish a short leader most of the time. I find it more effective to have my fly follow the fly line rather than ride above it. The exception is in the fall, when fish often stage in shallow water where a floating or intermediate sink line is required. Leader lengths are then dictated by the water depth.

**Flies:** Literally hundreds of fly patterns used for coho have worked at one time or another. That said, the development of patterns and their associated fishing methods is still in its infancy. Fortunately, over the years I have met several incredibly innovative saltwater fly tiers, and through the process of sharing ideas and adapting my techniques, a few patterns have evolved that are often successful. My favourites are Tim's Needlefish and Tim's Llama Needlefish, Herring, Sardine and Anchovy.

**Odds and sods:** A few things that should be with you to make the day *Tim's Blue Llama Anchovy*

*This 17–foot-long Boston Whaler is typical of the preferred style of open, unclut-tered boat that is popular for saltwater fly fishing.*

go smoothly are a good file or hook sharpener, polarized sunglasses, sun screen, clippers, needlenose pliers, an area marine chart, a tide guide, binoculars, a camera, lunch and drinking water.

**Boats:** An open boat is preferred, as fly casting with a cabin, sail or oth-er obstacles in your way is annoying. Add a little wind and rough water to the equation, and you have a great example of complete frustration.

As most of the fly fishing described here takes place on the west coast of Vancouver Island, a boat must be large enough and seaworthy enough to be safe in water with swells and some chop. If you don't have access to a good boat, or just want to get a feel for the experience and conditions, I recommend using an outfitter like Weigh West Marine Resort in Tofino. They have a fleet of well-equipped 17–foot Stinger boats designed specifically for fly fishing. Their operation also includes an on-the-water fish-master to keep you safe, locate fish, and help with fishing techniques.

# TECHNIQUES

**Finding coho:** The easiest place to start is by looking for bait. A good fish finder can save hours of searching, for you usually find bait well before marking coho. Likely places to explore are kelp beds, either right beside or in between them; beside or behind wash rocks; the slack side of tide lines; near underwater structures; under large foam patches; and in or on the edges of back eddies.

*When salmon are hard to find, moving in close to rocky outcrops and kelp beds is a good way to prospect for them.*

**Birds:** Spotting large concentrations of squawking gulls is a given, but don't forget to watch for small groups of diving birds. If one pops to the surface with a beak full of baitfish—bingo! Many days have been saved by watching them.

*"Wash rocks" like this one in Clayoquot Sound can be productive fishing locations anywhere around Vancouver Island.*

*"Bucktails" are often fashioned from polar bear hair or synthetics. They are meant for trolling, not casting, and often have a "stinger" hook in tandem for fish that strike short.*

*Bill Pollard's coho took a Tim's Llama Needlefish at BS Pass.*

**Bucktailing:** Trolling or "bucktailing" a fly covers a lot of water while hunting for action. A hookup indicates where the fish are, and by monitoring the fish finder you then stand a better chance of finding bait and salmon. Good places to bucktail are on flats in water 15 to 20 feet deep, and cuts or channels 20 to 50 feet deep.

To illustrate how search techniques can work in concert: Bill Pollard and I were exploring our usual haunts at "BS Pass" one August without much success, so we decided to bucktail. Soon after putting our lines in the water, we noticed two marbled murrelets surface with their beaks full of needlefish. As we turned and headed toward them, the fish finder lit up with a large school of needlefish at 30 feet. Needless to say, we reeled in and grabbed our fly rods armed with Tim's Llama Needlefish.

My first cast produced a subtle take, and on the set-up I felt a half-dozen hard throbs. An 8–pound coho cartwheeled about 20 feet from the boat and then streaked off. After three good runs and several impressive jumps, we finally slid the net under him. Bucktailing led us to the diving birds, which led us to the bait, which led us to a couple of hours of great fishing.

**Jumping fish:** Pay attention to jumping coho. If the spot where the jump occurred isn't too far away, cover the area while monitoring your sounder. Often, it's not a random jump, but a signal that feeding fish are around, and frequently with enough bait to keep them there for awhile.

One of the best trips I have ever experienced occurred the morning after a fabulous day spent fishing with Pollard. On the first day we had found coho next to a kelp bed bordering a favourite rock, and it seemed like we had fish on every minute of the day. We eagerly returned the following morning, but the bait and school of coho we had terrorized the day before were gone. A long, frustrating search of the area's kelp beds drew blanks. We were about to head elsewhere when Bill spotted a coho in the air about 200 feet out from the previous day's bonanza kelp bed. The screen on the fish finder produced an image that was truly unbelievable: we were in open water about 45 feet deep, without any visible kelp, structure or bait; however, a school of coho was stacked like cordwood at 42 feet. We anchored above the school and had a once-in-a-lifetime experience for the next four hours. The coho averaged two to four pounds larger than the previous day's fish, and they were even more aggressive. We lost track of the number caught and released, but did count the doubles that we landed—14.

*Casting and retrieving "downstream" from a wash rock often produces action, for baitfish gather in the slower-moving water.*

*What inshore saltwater fly fishing is all about. This hefty, chrome-bright coho is about to be released.*

**Fishing methods:** The majority of my fishing is done by casting upstream of the running tide, then counting the number of seconds required to get my fly near bottom. For example, a line with a seven–inch-per-second sink rate reaches 30 feet in 48 seconds.

With my fly at the desired depth, I start a slow, deliberate vertical retrieve with an approximate 12–inch stroke. I prefer fishing slowly,

*Tim Tullis with a by-product of fly fishing for coho one early September in Clayo-quot Sound. This 24–pound Chinook fell for a light blue Deceiver.*

as an injured or stunned baitfish is the easiest prey. Also, frightened needlefish will bury themselves in a sandy bottom; then, when the panic subsides they will gradually drift out of the sand and again become coho table fare.

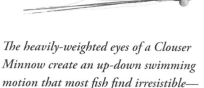

*The heavily-weighted eyes of a Clouser Minnow create an up-down swimming motion that most fish find irresistible—especially coho and Chinook salmon.*

Fish your fly right to the boat. Don't start your next cast until you can see your leader coming out of the water. Countless times I have had fish come from right under the boat to take my fly in only a few inches of water.

If you have fish around and conditions warrant it, or the slow retrieve is not working, don't hesitate to try other retrieves. For instance, if I have the opportunity to cover surface-slashing fish after a well-placed leading cast, I will usually take two or three long, rapid strokes before slowing down my fly. Fish will frequently hit my fly on the second or third stroke. This technique also works when fishing sand flats in depths of 15 to 20 feet.

Another method that works well at times is when anchored above a school of fish and the tide is running fairly heavy, cast upstream and allow your fly to get as deep as possible. Start the slow, deliberate retrieve, and after retrieving 12 feet or so, let your line slip back out and try it again.

An exception is when fishing a heavily-weighted fly like a Clouser Minnow, you may want to fish a faster retrieve to impart more action to the fly.

Remember—we must all pay our dues. So stay with it and you will have some fantastic fishing days. We, here on Vancouver Island, are extremely lucky to have a truly world class fishery right at our doorstep, which is what makes it such a great place to learn.

# OPEN OCEAN FLY PATTERNS

### Tim's Needlefish
*(Tim Tullis)*
**Hook:**    Mustad 34007, no. 1.
**Thread:**  3/0 clear UNI-Mono.
**Body:**    Medium diameter pearlescent braided Mylar tubing.
**Wing:**    Sparse polar bear hair or FisHair tied:

**No. 1:**
Olive green over 8–10 strands of
pearl Krystal Flash over white.

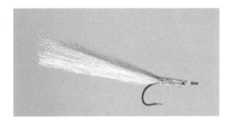

**No. 2:**
Blue over UV Pearl Krystal Flash
over white.

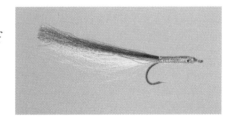

**No. 3:**
Purple over UV Pearl Krystal
Flash over white.

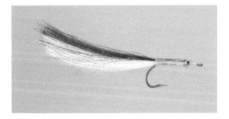

**Head:**    Medium diameter
           Mylar tubing length of shank.
**Eyes:**    3 mm adhesive Mylar, silver/black.
**Finish:**  Epoxy or Angler's Choice Soft Body.

**Tim's Llama Needlefish**
*(Tim Tullis)*
**Hook:** Eagle Claw Saltwater L067U–2, no. 2.
**Thread:** 4 mm clear UNI-Mono.

**No. 1:**
**Body:** Root's Llama Hair, medium green over white.
**Lateral line:** Root's Elite Flash mint green under 1 strand of silver Holographic Flashabou.

**No. 2:**
**Body:** Root's Llama Hair, golden olive over white.
**Lateral line:** Gold Polar Flash.

**Head:** Medium diameter Mylar tubing.
**Eyes:** 3 mm silver adhesive Mylar.
**Finish:** Epoxy or Anglers Choice Soft Body.

131

## Tim's Anchovy Needlefish
*(Tim Tullis)*

| | |
|---|---|
| **Hook:** | Eagle Claw L067U, no. 1. |
| **Thread:** | UNI-Mono. |
| **Belly:** | White Root's Llama Hair mixed with pearl/green enhancer. |
| **Sides:** | Bait Green Root's Llama Hair mixed with mint green enhancer. |
| **Back:** | Black Root's Llama Hair with 2–3 strands of black Flashabou, or use purple hair with purple Flashabou, or blue hair with blue Flashabou. |
| **Head:** | ⅜–inch length of small pearlescent braided Mylar tubing. |
| **Eyes:** | 4 mm silver adhesive Mylar |
| **Finish:** | Epoxy or Anglers Choice Soft Body. |

*Kamloops area trout guru Brian Chan loves saltwater fly fishing, and practices it whenever the chance is presented.*

*Author Tim Tullis had no trouble in adjusting from Interior rainbow trout fly fishing to inshore coho and chinook salmon.*

Qualicum Beach resident **Tim Tullis** manages the Surfside RV Resort in Parksville. Prior to that he owned and operated Hatheume Lake Resort for 22 years in the Interior. He started fly fishing at 8, tying flies at 10, and selling them at 12 to support his fishing and tying habit. Several of his Interior patterns remain in popular use, and his saltwater patterns are following suit. Tim's other claims to fame are that he served as president of the Evergreen Fly Fishers in Everett, Washington, and is a founding charter member and the first president of both The Lonely Loon (Kelowna) and the Mid-Island Castaways fly fishing clubs.

# CHAPTER TEN

*Perfect fly-fishing conditions include high slack tide and no wind.*

# DREDGING FOR
# BOTTOM FISH *by Robert H. Jones*

135

There are die-hard inshore fly fishers who get fixated on salmon—usually coho—and nothing else matters. Ever. And when the fish simply aren't present, or have developed lockjaw for whatever reason, these enthusiasts stay locked irrevocably onto their pursuit of silver fish. The rest of us let our flies sink down toward bottom and see if we can entice a colourful greenling, toothy lingcod or pug-ugly cabezon into livening up the day for a few minutes.

Bottom fishing hardly ranks up there with brain surgery or applied mathematics. They are called bottom fish (also ground fish) for the very obvious reason that this is where they are usually found. Ergo, to catch them you must present your hook-laden offering within their range. The most efficient method of accomplishing this is with a heavy metal jig and strong, small diameter line—say a one–pound Gibbs Mudraker

*While low slack tide means less water depth to reach bottom, some feel that the bite is not as intensive as during high slack.*

dangling from 80–pound-test Stren Superbraid line. The solid metal lure is heavy and compact, so sinks rapidly, and the line's small diameter means it will be less affected by surface tension from tidal currents, which tends to lift even a one–pound lure up off the bottom.

Now, if this sounds like the exact opposite of a nearly weightless fly trailing from the end of a large diameter fly line you're quite right. Therefore, two important points must be considered in order to get your fly down where it will attract attention: time and location. The general rule for jigging is that the prime time is about 30 minutes before, during, and after a slack tide. This because the tidal current is slowing as it nears high or low slack, and then starts increasing slowly as it begins to flood. The same holds true for presenting a fly on the bottom, but only to a degree. This is where location figures into the equation—the shallower the better. Because the current cre-

ates surface tension on your fly line, the deeper the water, the less you can rely on getting down to the bottom, especially during that half-hour before and after slack. This means that your best window of opportunity is during the slack period itself, but bear in mind that even then there is always some current present.

Many, me included, prefer high slack, but low slack definitely provides an edge on water depth. Obviously, reaching bottom in 20 feet of water is much easier and faster than in 60 feet, which is about the maximum most of us can fish comfortably, and then only under ideal conditions.

If there is no wind, you can drift freely and cast, but even a slow drift will belly your line up toward the surface. In most cases you are better off to anchor or tie up to a kelp bed. This usually has the added attraction of putting you in position for

*Standard salmon-weight tackle works well for most bottom fishing situations, especially black rock-fish like this dandy landed by Jack Simpson.*

*Olive Clouser Minnow*

*Cameron's Copper Clouser*

*Weigh West Clouser*

a mixed bag of greenling, lingcod, cabezon, flounders, various types of rockfish, and possibly even a halibut. Sometimes you might even encounter a Chinook or coho salmon, but I don't ever recall any anglers complaining about this.

Tackle requirements are simply whatever you happen to be using for salmon, which in most cases is an 8–weight outfit of nine to 10½ feet long, along with the fastest-sinking line you can cast easily. A word to the wise: ensure that your line is squeaky clean, because you will be making long casts.

I usually carry a few "flexible sinkers" fashioned from lead-core, braided nylon trolling line. These range from three to six feet long, and when strung between the fly line and leader butt occasionally mean the difference between reaching bottom or not. These are easily fashioned from 20–pound test line by sliding the outer sheath back to expose about four inches of lead wire and then pinching it off. The tag end is then folded to form a loop, and bound tightly with wraps of fine nylon thread. After repeating on the opposite end, a coat of flexible cement or Pliobond protects the thread wraps.

For years I have maintained that the only fly required for bottom fish is a Clouser Minnow in one of its many guises. They have an enticing up-down-up-down swimming action that attracts fish, but another important feature is that the hook point rides upward, thereby avoiding most obstructions. Also, when the hook is set, the point pulls directly up into the upper jaw, which is a plus when fishing a long line.

A proper Clouser is tied very skimpy and slim, but for bottom fish you can beef up the dressing as much as desired, and make them all sorts of bright, garish colours and combinations thereof. I tie most of mine on Tiemco 9394, no. 2 hooks, which is as large as required, and use large-sized lead dumbbell eyes.

If anchoring or tying up to a kelp bed, do so from the bow, then fish one angler from the bow and one from the stern. The most effective tactic for getting down is what I call the "slack line drop." Cast out as far as you can comfortably, then strip another 30 to 40 feet of line from your reel and let it lay in loose coils on the deck or, better yet, in a plastic tub or box to prevent it from hanging up or getting stepped on. Strip in the line, then cast your fly "upstream" into the current and quickly shake the remainder of the slack line through the guides. This allows it to sink in a more level configuration rather than swing down like a pendulum.

A good way to judge how deep you are getting is to compare the

*The edge of a kelp bed is a prime location for tying up or anchoring from the bow.*

depth indicated on the depth sounder to the length of your cast. Assuming, of course, that you know how far you can cast. What many anglers think is an 80–foot cast often measures about 20 feet shorter.

If the sounder reads 60 feet and you are casting 60 feet, your fly won't reach bottom because of the line bellying; however, shaking that loose line through the guides after each cast allows it to get down there and remain close to the bottom over a reasonable distance. You will know it's there when you feel it drag and bump against obstructions. The length of time it remains down and the distance it covers depends on variables like the line's diameter and density, water depth, current speed, and whether or not a fish grabs it.

Strip in line just fast enough to stay in touch with the fly, giving it occasional erratic twitches, until it hangs perpendicular from the rod tip. Then, as it travels past the boat, pay out loose line again. When the

*After making your cast "upstream" in the current, shake loose line through the guides.*

*Flounder are often found in shallow water with a sandy bottom.*

drift has ended, let the current belly the line and lift your fly upward, for fish will swim up after it, often for surprising distances—even flatfish like flounder and halibut.

One of my favourite bottom fish is flounder, which are often found in fairly shallow water (15 to 20 feet); are amazingly strong and active for their size; and taste so good when pan fried. They are such eager biters that catching them is simply a matter of finding them—and where you find one you will usually find an abundance of them, and usually of similar size.

If unfamiliar with the waters, use your depth sounder to look for a flat, sandy bottom at depths of 20 to 60 feet, and then drag a Clouser Minnow right on the bottom. A 12–inch-long flounder will outpull most freshwater fish of equal weight. Hook into a 16– or 18–incher and you will really have your hands full. Even on 8–weight tackle they can be a lot of fun.

Saltwater fly fishers pursuing salmon often encounter black rockfish, especially on the west coast of Vancouver Island and in Queen Charlotte Strait. They often school right on the surface, where they can be taken on poppers and hair bugs. On a day when Chinooks seem non-existent and coho are playing hard to get, encountering a school of blacks can really liven up an otherwise slow day. Unlike deeper-swimming rockfish, lightly-hooked blacks taken under these circumstances

*Ralph Shaw with a rock sole (left) and a mottled sand dab (right).*

can be released without worrying about whether or not they will recover. Unfortunately, copper and brown rockfish, the two most other common species, do not fare as well. If a fish shows the least sign of distress, it should be retained, staying within the daily bag limit, of course.

Although lingcod have been recorded at weights exceeding 100 pounds, the average taken in inshore waters is about 8–20 pounds. They are strong, determined fighters that put up excellent accounts for themselves. Although considered outstanding eating, the smaller fish are your best choice. Large fish—anything much beyond 15 pounds—are usually spawning-age females, so releasing them makes good sense from a conservation point of view.

Greenlings are smaller relatives of lingcod. Four species are common to British Columbia waters: painted, rock, whitespotted and kelp. Of these, the latter is most common. Amazingly swift and strong for their size, kelp greenling usually peak at 21 inches—about three pounds. The male is medium olive-brown in colour, with irregular-shaped turquoise markings around the head and shoulders. Females are lighter, almost reddish brown, covered with dark brown spots, and have an orange hue to their fins. Not as common, rock greenlings grow to 24 inches. Their colour ranges from brown to greenish, with irregular bright crimson stripes along the sides. All greenling are excellent table fare.

Cabezon is Spanish for "big head"—which accounts for about ⅓ of their body mass. Mottled brownish green in colour, they have a large mouth with huge, rubbery lips, and their pectoral fins are of about the

*Mottled sand dabs are easily identified because of their orange spots.*

same diameter as the head. When flared, they make a cabezon appear as wide as it is long. These largest members of the sculpin family are probably the homeliest fish you will ever catch on a fly, but rest assured that you will get your money's worth. Recorded to weights of 30 pounds, they average about 8 to 20 pounds. Even the smaller ones possess the size, strength and stamina to guarantee memorable encounters. Although the flesh is of good quality and taste, the roe is extremely toxic.

Although halibut tend to be deep-water fish, they occasionally frequent water shallow enough that they can be targeted with flies. This is certainly the case in Clayoquot Sound and Kyuquot Sound, which leads me to believe that most sounds on the west coast of Vancouver Island offer similar situations.

A friend once told me of fly fishing for coho in Alaska, when he and a friend hooked several halibut of 15 to 35 pounds on flies. Although they were in 90 feet of water, all of their coho and halibut action was at 30 feet. Nevertheless, if intentionally targeting halibut, you stand a better chance presenting your fly on or near the bottom.

Pound for pound, halibut are as strong as Chinook salmon. They won't run as fast, but they are no slouches, and runs of 100 to 200 yards or more are quite possible. Thus, if targeting halibut (or big lingcod for that matter), use a minimum of 10–weight tackle, with 12–weight an option. A reel loaded with at least 200 yards of 30–pound test backing, 100 feet of running line, and a 600 grain shooting head. A 20–pound

143

*Martin Paish with a black rockfish that took his chartreuse Clouser Minnow while he was casting for coho.*

*This dandy lingcod took Martin Paish's chartreuse Clouser Minnow as he was fishing it close to the bottom.*

test leader will probably suffice, and you might want to up the hook size to no. 2/0 or so.

Look for areas where the bottom is relatively flat and preferably covered with sand or gravel. Halibut also frequent rocky, uneven bottoms, but you increase the probability of hanging up on obstructions. Clayoquot Sound and Kyuquot Sound have several places around their outer islands and shoals where halibut are taken in fairly shallow water—40 to 60 feet—so it's simply a matter of studying a marine chart of an area.

Fly fishing for bottom fish isn't for everyone, and that's just fine for those of us who enjoy it. However, if you haven't tried it, don't knock it, for it can be a lot of fun—and that's what fly fishing's all about.

# BOTTOM FLY PATTERN

**Clouser Minnow**
*(Bob Clouser) Robert H. Jones*

| | |
|---|---|
| **Hook:** | Tiemco 93944XL, no.2 |
| **Thread:** | 6/0 UNI-Thread, red and chartreuse. |
| **Eyes:** | Large dumbbells, lead or substitute, bound tightly to shank with figure–8 wraps of red thread. Apply a drop of Krazy Glue to lock in position. |
| **Belly:** | White bucktail, polar bear hair or synthetic. Tie in with red thread, then cross rearward between the eyes and create a narrow band (gills) around the hair and shank. Cut off red thread. Turn hook upside down in vise and lock chartreuse thread at the head. |
| **Lateral line:** | 15–20 strands of Krystal Flash about ⅛–inch longer than back and belly hair. |
| **Back:** | Chartreuse bucktail, polar bear hair or Synthetic. Do not wrap lateral line or back behind the eyes. |

*Robin Pike with a colourful female kelp greenling that took his—you guessed it—Chartreuse Clouser Minnow.*

# INDEX

## TACTICS
  beach fishing, 45
  bucktailing, 126
  fan casting, 49
  open-ocean fly fishing, 119,
      120
  trolling flies, 27, 95
  vertical retrieve, 128
  wash rocks, 125
  wet-line anglers, 24, 25

# More Great Books From Harbour Publishing

## COASTAL FISHES OF THE PACIFIC NORTHWEST

*Coastal Fishes of the Pacific Northwest* is the only comprehensive field guide to marine fishes of BC, Washington, and southern Alaska and includes a brief but detailed description of each fish's habitat, physical characteristics and behaviour—everything that a fisherman or an amateur naturalist needs to know.
*Andy Lamb and Phil Edgell · 0-920080-75-8 · Paperback · 5.5 x 8.5*

## LAKE, RIVER AND SEA-RUN FISHES OF CANADA

The only complete guide to freshwater game fishes in all parts of Canada, this book is a must for naturalists, anglers and everyone wanting to know more about Canada's wildlife. *Lake, River and Sea-Run Fishes of Canada* offers biology, angling tips and notes on the curiosities of all the best-known game fishes, and fishing lore from high mountain lakes, prairie rivers, the Great Lakes, the Arctic coastline and ocean tide pools.
*Frederick H. Wooding · 1-55017-175-5 · Paperback · 6 x 9*

## MARINE LIFE OF THE PACIFIC NORTHWEST:

A Photographic Encyclopedia of Invertebrates, Seaweeds and Selected Fishes
With 1,700 superb colour photographs, *Marine Life of the Pacific Northwest* allows the reader to recognize coastal organisms found from southern Alaska to northern California. Each species is identified with photographs and includes a description with information on range, habitat, appearance and behaviour.
*Andy Lamb and Bernard P. Hanby · 1-55017-361-8 · Hardcover · 8.5 x 11*

Available at better bookstores and from
**Harbour Publishing,**
P.O. Box 219, Madeira Park, BC, V0N 2H0
Toll-free order line 1-800-667-2988
Toll-free fax order line 1-877-604-9449
Email orders@harbourpublishing.com
www.harbourpublishing.com